PN Review 241

VOLUME 44   NUMBER 5   MAY–JUNE 2(

0 **Stella Halkyard** Pictures from a Library   02 **Editorial**   03 **News & Notes**
83 **Contributors**   85 **Michael Powell** From Chetham's Library

REPORTS

05 **Vahni Capildeo**
Report from Fife

06 **Jamie Osborn**
Letter from Brussels

07 **Natasha Stallard**
on Sylvia Plath

08 **Sam Adams**
Letter from Wales

09 **Neil Astley**
on Helen Dunmore

10 **James Womack**
Letter from Washington

11 **Beverley Bie Brahic**
Darning

12 **Marius Kociejowski**
from The Notebooks

14 **Frank Kuppner**
A Few Offhand Remarks

ON THE COVER
Owen Gent,
'Icarus No. 2'

Curator: Valgerður
Þóroddsdóttir.

POEMS & FEATURES

15 **Kei Miller**
the Fat Black Woman

20 **Parwana Fayyaz**
Four Poems

23 **Gabriel Josipovici**
Aharon Appelfeld

26 **Craig Raine**
A Sequence and Six
Poems

31 **Vidyan Ravinthiran**
on A. R. Ammons

34 **Ian Pople**
on A. R. Ammons

37 **Maryann Corbett**
Two Poems

38 **Kristín Ómarsdóttir**
Eight Poems
(*trans. Vala Thorodds*)

40 **Fiona Moore**
Three Poems

43 **Duncan MacKay**
on Charles Olson

45 **Robert Minhinnick**
Two Poems

46 **Tim Murdoch**
Four Poems

47 **Barry Wood**
on Rich and Pound

51 **Ashley Anna McHugh**
Four Poems

53 **C. K. Stead**
on Allen Curnow

58 **Nicholas Friedman**
Three Poems

59 **Mark Valentine**
Five Poems

60 **Edwin Morgan**
Translator's Notebook
(*ed. James McGonigal*)

64 **Leo Boix**
Five Poems

REVIEWS

66 **Ruth Hawthorn**
on Robert Lowell

67 **Tony Roberts**
on James Wright

68 **Sasha Dugdale**
on Nuar Alsadir and
Leontia Flynn

70 **Alison Brackenbury**
on Enitharmon Press

71 **Phoebe Power**
on Kayo Chingonyi and
Ocean Vuong

73 **Sue Leigh**
on Fleur Adcock

74 **Rory Waterman**
on Douglas Dunn

75 **Adam Heardman**
on Sinéad Morrisey

76 **Rowland Bagnall**
on Luke Kennard

77 **Hilary Davies**
on Michael Symmons
Roberts

78 **Joey Connolly**
on Three Poets

80 **Will Maclean**
on Bryce and Keung

81 **Valerie Duff**
on Dan Beachy-Quick

82 **Jane Draycott**
on Five Pamphlets

Editorial

CHARLES BUKOWSKI SAID, or is said to have said, lots of pithy things. They can be found on web sites such as addicted2success.com, side by side with 'Great Lessons You Can Learn from Theodore Roosevelt' and other sustaining gobbets from Grant Cardone ('Don't Just Make Money, Make a Difference'), Lori Greiner, Kendrick Lamar, Andy Frisella, Mark Zuckerberg, Michael B. Jordan, Justin Timberlake, Meryl Streep. Streep has said no fewer than thirty-two 'remarkable things', including, 'You can't get spoiled if you do your own ironing.' Bukowski scores '14 Thought-Provoking Life Quotes', rather below par in this context. On goodreads.com he scores well over two thousand, some of them quite long and several with over one thousand 'likes'. 'Without literature, life is hell' gets one thousand and twenty-three. One quote gets no votes at all, though it merits a few:

> Yes, I know what you mean about writing and writers. We seem to have lost the target. Writers seem to write to be known as writers. They don't write because something is driving them toward the edge. I look back at when Pound, T. S. Eliot, e. e. Cummings, Jeffers, Auden, Spender were about. Their work cracked right through the paper, set it on fire. Poems became events, explosions. There was a high excitement. Now, for decades there has seemed to be this lull, almost a practiced lull, as if dullness indicated genius. And if a new talent came along it was only a flash, a few poems, a thin book and then he or she was sanded down, ingested into the quiet nothingness. Talent without durability is a god damned crime. It means they went to the soft trap, it means they believed the praise, it means they settled short. A writer is not a writer because he has written some books. A writer is not a writer because he teaches literature. A writer is only a writer if he can write now, tonight, this minute. We have too many x-writers who type. Books fall from my hand to the floor. They are total crap. I think we have just blown away half a century to the stinking winds. Yes.

Bukowski (1920–94), described by his publisher John Martin as 'the new Walt Whitman', is in the news again a quarter of a century after his death. The occasion is his posthumous poetry, an almost inexhaustible supply (he wrote copiously every day), and the outrageous news – not new, but now widely publicised – that his very longtime, faithful, long-suffering publisher, founder of Black Sparrow Press, had used the poet's absence due to death as an occasion to edit the poems he added to the *oeuvre* in ways Bukowski would have resisted, and Linda Bukowski, his widow, has on his behalf. In a 2013 blog Michael Philips blew the whistle with a piece called 'The senseless, tragic rape of Charles Bukowski's ghost by John Martin's Black Sparrow Press'. This blog, with prequels and sequels, is a fascinating study, fundamentalist in its hostility to editorial intervention in creative work.

Michael Hofmann in *PNR* in 1986 reviewed Bukowski's Black Sparrow *War All The Time: Poems 1981–1984*, which weighed in at three hundred pages and was only the tiny tip of that four-year iceberg. We read, 'Buk dishing it out to Mexicans, women, writers, critics, remembering his postman days, going out to the races and restaurants, commenting on his fame and the things that accompany it.' Bukowski is always accessible. 'The writing makes no great claims or demands, it gives itself up readily enough to the speed-reader, having itself been written at speed...'

John Martin, ten years Bukowski's junior, published most of his work, setting up Black Sparrow for that purpose, paying Bukowski a retainer and encouraging him into fiction. Martin's list came to include Paul Bowles, John Fante, Robert Duncan, Denise Levertov, Charles Reznikoff and many others. In 2002 Martin disposed of the press in two lots. Bukowski and the crown jewels went to Ecco, the bulk of the rich backlist to David Godine.

The poems Martin is accused of vandalising were those rejected from the books Martin and Bukowski assembled in the poet's lifetime. Black Sparrow tried to keep faith with the ghost of Bukowski by sifting and re-sifting the manuscript remains, panning the dross. In Martin's view the uncollected work had to come up to snuff or its publication might damage Bukowski's reputation. His impulse was the opposite of vandalism, though his judgement may have been at fault. Philips claims the 'Wholesale removal of references to drinking, drugs, sex and madness', trademark themes. (Quite a lot of drinking, drugs, sex and madness survive.) Even readers not keen on Bukowski can see that Martin's revisions are not invariably improvements.

Could it be that Martin's strategy was to adjust the received impression of Bukowski so that, as the tides of critical fashion and theoretical censure shift, the poet who was 'unafraid', in Abel Debritto's description, and 'talked about anything and everything, as if taboo and fear were not part of his vocabulary', might be in danger of losing his readership? 'Smiling, he unleashed all kinds of hell on the blank page. He deliberately came up with this tough guy image, this Dirty Old Man persona that attracted and repulsed readers equally.' Dirty Old Men have less currency than they once did. Martin was a publisher: he could read the runes. 'Having little time for double standards, Bukowski punched readers in the gut,' says Debritto approvingly, 'hit them hard with his trademark uppercuts, making them feel each and every word on the page, spare and simple as they were.' This language, like Bukowski's, is unreflectingly gendered. Integrity would appear to entail unrestrained self-expression, regardless of whose gut is being punched.

The *Los Angeles Review of Books* (2 March 2018) featured Debritto's substantial article on the topic. With chapter and quite a bit of verse, he makes the case. In his indignation, he does not consider what might have motivated Martin in making the changes. He puts Martin with Maxwell Perkins, who wrestled Thomas Wolfe into shape and engaged with Hemingway and Fitzgerald; and Gordon Lish, who helped make (it seems to some readers) rather than mar Raymond Carver. There are less literate and more righteous editors, too, who 'change works back' on the authority of writers' manuscripts, even when the writers have agreed to edits. Such editors find integrity only in 'first thought best thought' (Ginsberg's phrase).

Eleven collections appeared in Bukowski lifetime; twelve (one thousand six hundred poems) still under Martin's aegis, followed his death. Among the mass of Bukowski's manuscripts Martin no doubt made errors. He brought the books out, however; the poet stayed news. No other publisher would have had the patience, authority or means to support Bukowski as Martin did. When Debritto, a card-carrying Bukowski fan, says that 'Bukowski's original beauty is simply gone' from the posthumous books, he forgets that the books themselves collect work that lacked the 'original beauty' and was excluded from titles published in the poet's lifetime.

Michael Philips's 2013 blog and the *Los Angeles Review of Books* article give telling examples of the changes introduced between manuscript and publication. Martin selected the content of Bukowski's poetry books when the poet was alive. He did not rewrite, but he organised and shaped them. His part in Bukowski's poems and fiction is central. He is part of a process that, as with so many writers, is *collaboration*. Admirers of Bukowski owe Martin a debt. When they cry 'rape' they unwrite literary history.

Ecco has published a new posthumous collection, *Storm for the Living and the Dead*, copied unedited from Bukowski's scripts. It is an economy for a publisher not to edit. New purists celebrate: this patch of tapestry need not be unwoven. But when it comes to it, they cannot unweave the larger texture of Bukowski's poetry, in which Martin's contribution is part of the very fibre.

News & Notes

Lucie Brock-Broido · The eccentric, brittle, reclusive American poet Lucie Brock-Broido died in March at the age of sixty-one. She avoided 'the real world' and in her poetry created a world in some respects more vertiginous and unaccountable than the world she sidestepped. Stanley Kunitz noted her 'taste for the fantastic' and her 'brilliant *nervosity*', a wonderfully accurate and unexpected term for a certain kind of fearful, trembling, attent alertness. She described her own style as 'feral'.

She published four books of poems which add up to a coherent *oeuvre*; there is a sense of a writer going deeper rather than forward, in the manner of her beloved Emily Dickinson whose example loomed large for her, especially in her second book, *The Master Letters*. Despite an instinct for reclusiveness, she was a Director of Poetry in the School of the Arts at Columbia University and taught previously at Harvard, the Bennington Writing Seminars and Princeton. She received awards from the John Simon Guggenheim Foundation, the National Endowment for the Arts and the American Academy of Arts and Letters.

Deborah Garrison, Brock-Broido's editor at Knopf, told the *New York Times* in an email: 'she went deeper into herself, into grief, and into the hard work of growing older'. Her poem 'Two Girls Ago', a resonant sequel to 'A Girl Ago', from *Stay, Illusion* (Knopf, 2013) suggests a tense survival:

> No exquisite instruments.
> No dead coming back as wrens in rooms at dawn.
> No suicidal hankering; no hankering for suicide.
> No one thousand days.
> No slim luck for the only President I ever loved.
> No lukewarm bath in oatmeal.
> No lantern left for Natalie on the way home from school in her
> Alaskan dark.
> No eye.
> No Victorian slippers that walked the bogs to moor.
> No Donner bones with cuts on them or not.
> No horizontal weeping; no weeping vertically.
> No flipping back your black tails at the black piano bench.
> No Elgar, no Tallis, no post-industrial despair.
> No French kissing in the field of wild raspberry and thorn.
> No commissioned urn.
> No threat. In the table of contents I'm not dead yet.

Zbigniew Herbert Literary Award · On 5 March it was announced that the Gaelic poet Nuala Ní Dhomhnaill had been awarded the 2018 Zbigniew Herbert International Literary Award for 2018, the first woman to be so honoured. She was characterised as 'a female hero' of a 'small language'. The chairman of the judges, the American poet Ed Hirsch, declared: 'We have chosen a ground-breaking and courageous poet who is both local and international, a poet, who has helped to sustain and remake her language.' The judging panel, truly international, includes also Yurii Andrukhovych (Ukraine), Michael Krüger (Germany), Mercedes Montana (Spain) and Tomas Różycki (Poland). The award has been presented since 2013, commemorating the great Polish poet and essayist, and previous recipients include the Americans W.S. Merwin and Charles Simic, the Pole Ryszard Krynicki, the Swede Lars Gustafsson and the South African and French citizen Breyten Breytenbach.

Raymond Danowski · A curious obituary in the *New York Times* introduced readers to Raymond Danowski, dead at seventy-four, described as a 'stockpiler of poetry', whose personal collection of tens of thousands of volumes was donated to the Emory University, Georgia and formed the basis of its remarkable collection and archive of modern poetry. 'Reading,' says the *New York Times*, 'was the lifeline that enabled Raymond Danowski to escape the smothering grip of a Bronx public housing project and an abusive father, so when Mr Danowski grew older, both rhyme and reason prompted him to stockpile books of poetry voraciously.' His library reached seventy-five thousand volumes. It lived for a time in Hertfordshire, then in London and Geneva, and finally, in 2004, it arrived at Emory 'cramm[ed] into four boxcar-size shipping containers'. There they are known collectively as the 'Raymond Danowski Poetry Library'. 'He was introduced to poetry by two uncles,' said the *Times*, 'one an aspiring actor who flamboyantly performed Edgar Allan Poe's "The Raven" at home, and another whose English bookie mailed him poems by W. H. Auden. (Mr Danowski ultimately collected about a thousand volumes of Auden's works.)' Why Emory? 'Because it was expanding its poetry archive (since 1975 it had acquired the papers of Seamus Heaney and Ted Hughes) and agreed to make Mr Danowski's *"bibliotheque imaginaire"* available not only to scholars but also to undergraduates.'

Wu Ming-yi · Late in March, the Taiwanese writer Wu Ming-yi was shortlisted for the Man Booker International Prize. On the Man Booker website, the judges (or site editors) re-named his country 'Taiwan, China', occasioning a protest from the author and his publishers. The change was made without reference to him. His book *The Stolen Bicycle* was one of thirteen novels shortlisted. 'Over the past few months,' the Central News Agency reported, 'pressure from China caused name changes for Taiwan on the web sites of overseas institutions from hotels and airlines to the Swedish tax authorities.' It was announced early in April that the Man Booker website had been amended and the novelist returned to Taiwan proper.

'*Pure Hollywood* is pure gold. Come for the art of her exquisitely weird writing and stay for the human drama.'
Ottessa Moshfegh

PRAISE FOR CHRISTINE SCHUTT

'Pared down but rich, dense, fevered, exactly right and eerily beautiful.'
John Ashbery

'A truly gifted writer.'
George Saunders

Available for pre-order now and purchase from 10 May 2018
www.andotherstories.org/book/pure-hollywood

www.andotherstories.org
@andothertweets
andotherstoriesbooks
@andotherpics

Access the entire *PN Review* archive with Exact Editions

Launched as *Poetry Nation*, a twice-yearly hardback, in 1973, *PN Review* began quarterly publication in 1976 and has appeared six times a year since *PN Review* 1981.

Visit www.pnreview.co.uk for more information

Report from Fife

VAHNI CAPILDEO

StAnza, Scotland's International Poetry Festival, took place from 7 to 11 March at St Andrews this year. The theme – 'Borderlines and the Self' – was interpreted both freely and literally, from the 'Poetry Selves: Tattoos, Masks and Moustaches' available at the festival desk (scarlet and violet alternative faces now hang above my bed), to the labels on plants, and on the wintry lack or promise of plants, in the parterres of the Preservation Trust Museum Garden, in Gerry Loose's 'A Rose is a Rose is a' creation.

Borderlines and the self are susceptible to being frail and lateral, as well as free or literal. Some of the interpretations served sterner functions; at the Imprisoned Poets Reading, Scottish PEN had placed an empty chair on the stage. The bodily presence of the poets who stood to read from the work of writers who cannot attend literary festivals, because their liberty is violently denied them, served to activate the emptiness of the chair. The chair was with in being without: sitting there with and alongside these solid, breathing speakers of words, in being without and remote from those others who had originated the word. Signifying more than absence and denial, the simple, unoccupied frame bespoke solidarity and desire. Alone, it was an occupation. It was a humbling reminder that quibbles over, for example, whether actors should read poets' work (for which the Forward Prizes received criticism) or whether poets need to double down on sincerity, double up their competencies, and act as performers (about which I have nothing to say in these pages), are perhaps distractions from the transmissibility of the word.

A festival like StAnza, as several happy people were heard to remark, is unafraid of interweaving languages other than Scots and English. StAnza participants and attendees revel in multilingualism, and enjoy harking back to other encounters between languages and literatures. We recalled such encounters and performances, at StAnza or elsewhere, and by this process of recollection, folded those appreciations into what was happening in StAnza's poetic present. StAnza memories played on continuous personal and shared loops, in a way akin to the public installations, which not only brought voices from Flanders and the Netherlands, but also Pamela Breda's transformations of the rhythms of plants into sound, and recordings from global poets from StAnzas past.

Nuala Ni Dhomnaill created a mini-loop of appreciative attention by explaining her technique of reading English versions before reading her Irish poems; she knew that that few of her listeners had access to the Irish, but believed that this way round, we would bring an altered and intensified quality of listening to each poem's second instantiation as more than pure music of untranslated syllable. This reminded me, by contrast, of a no less good but different recitation that I had seen in London a few years ago, where the opposite decision was taken by a Farsi poet and his translator; the reason and the result being that the kinetic and declamatory aspects of the Farsi poet's presentation came to the fore.

A Scottish writer in my workshop on the late Jamaican writer Anthony McNeill volunteered to read McNeill's dramatic poem 'Who's Sammy' aloud, after I pointed out that my now messed-up, originally southern Antillean accent could not do and never would have done it justice. It was eerie for me to hear McNeill so voiced: the placement of the tongue, lips, and palate pursing or opening out the vowels, the faint rhoticity colouring the r's. Just through a simple recitation, I noticed more piercingly than ever before, the real if vexed kinship of the Jamaican and the Scottish in speech as well as blood.

A love of both the formal or linguistic shaping, and the suggestive or alinguistic manifestation, of sound – utterance's selving, aural selvedge – permitted transcendent moments, in 2018 as before. Thanks to Rachael Boast's extraordinary reading voice and her presentation, with co-readers, of her and Andy Ching's tribute anthology, W. S. Graham's sea seemed to thunder and whisper from the stairs of the J. G. & Innes bookshop, as if filling dry corners and uncorking inks. A number of festival-goers also harked back to the beautiful irruption of Occitan song into Aurélia Lassaque's discussion at StAnza 2017. Throughout, the oysterish light of the north pearled through the artists' books and installations curated by Julie Johnstone in 'each breath, a page / each page, a breath', seen or unseen, placed on a windowsill and on a table in the Preservation Trust Museum.

Some festivals demand to be inhabited as if they are a cult space, or lived through as if they are an endurance test, poetry versions of corporate 'away days', with their irregular and expensive comforts offered to bolster an experience of traumatic and silly bonding. Not this one. The energy running through the streets around the Byre and the other sites was generated by a sense of human connection. It could be said that the StAnza 2018 theme of 'borderlines and the self' was being realised via a kind of collective activity, as well as through the programmed or green-flash transformations within and between languages and arts. I gathered that those who return to StAnza often look forward to seeing friends there whom otherwise they might not have seen since the previous year. This reminded me of ancient pilgrimage sites, long trails across the quarrelsome borders of principalities and geographies, with stops where meetings with others who can no longer count as strangers, since they are also engaged on at least partly the same journey, recur or can be contemplated as recurrent.

Naturally the feeling of any festival has its source in the life that people have been living around, before and after it. Perhaps I should mention how my StAnza 2018 was bracketed: by the birds in my friends Madeleine and Stuart's garden, the site where I had learnt to identify yellowhammers and now was learning to distinguish tree sparrows from house sparrows; where only glass, and sometimes not even that, separated us at meals, from what had been eight pheasants, now six, since the thawing of the profound and terrible snows; where no pastoral made it possible to forget the other singing which had been happening on university pickets during the strike. How precarity and survivability walk the line.

Letter from Brussels

Jamie Osborn

I

In September 2017, the Belgian minister for asylum and migration, Theo Francken, announced the arrest of fourteen African migrants in Brussels' Parc Maximilien. Posting on Facebook, he celebrated the news with the hashtag #opkuisen – '*opkuisen*', in Flemish, meaning a particularly unpleasant clean-up, ridding oneself of filth. Forced to defend himself, he claimed he had meant to refer to the 'problems' not to 'people'.

A protest was called outside the Office des Étrangers, opposite the park. The chants could be heard several hundred metres down the street, despite the relatively small crowd. *Première, deuxième, troisième génération, nous sommes tous les enfants des immigrés! So! So! So! Solidarité! Avec les sans-papiers!* From the knot of people – spiky-haired women with the usual badges (*Bread not bombs*, *Nuke-free zone*, *Boycott Israeli APARTHEID!*), an enormously fat man with the loudspeaker, two children holding hands – bikes jutted out into the street and formed a barrier against cars passing too close. I kissed on the cheek an artist I had met a few days earlier, who would meet no one's gaze and was constantly flicking her eyes from buildings to ground to sky so they reflected grey, brown, blue. Up against the park fence on the other side of the street was a handful of migrants, watching with curious or stony expressions. A dozen or so police officers stood round the doors of the building and beside their vans, in soft blue fleecy jackets, with guns that looked too ostentatious to be real.

Drummers arrived, beginning softly, then working up to a more aggressive rhythm. A policewoman reached out to stop a child about to run into the street and led her back to her mother. The chants began to change: *Theo – fascio! Police – collabo!* A ripple went through the crowd. Why were the police still smiling? Opposition shone in the protestors' eyes.

Across the street, the composition of the group of onlookers had altered. Without being able to say who or when, some faces had gone, others had arrived. After a time, five young men leapt the fence and joined in singing; the others shifted to fill their space.

I left with the artist. She wheeled her bike into the middle of the road and deliberately – very much a body, a problem and a human – paraded in front of a bus that was forced to trail behind her and add its honking to the chants.

II

A short time later, Francken played host to Sudanese government officials come to help Belgian migration officers identify people to deport. There were public warnings that people returned to Sudan would be at risk of torture; Francken rejected this and when questioned would only respond that he had 'a working relationship with the Sudanese authorities'. The Belgian administration put out pictures of a grinning Francken shaking hands with the Sudanese ambassador, Mustrif Siddiq (who happens to be the former director of the Sudanese secret services). Other pictures emerged, grainier, shot under cover, of hooded migrants being hoarded onto a bus in the middle of the night.

In December, a leaked letter that had been sent earlier in the year by the Commissioner General for Asylum and Stateless Persons proved that Francken knew there was a definite risk of torture, contrary to what he had told the Federal Parliament. For a time, it looked as though Francken might be dismissed, following public protests, but pressure from his Flemish nationalist N-VA party, ensured he kept his post and the Prime Minister Charles Michel posted on Facebook a statement calling for 'nuance' and claiming to 'put the dots on the i's' concerning the facts.

My artist friend brought forward the opening of her exhibition to respond to the events. In the first room, a sodden dome tent patched with blankets and plastic sheeting squatted in the middle of the floor. Beams of torchlight flashed into the viewers' faces and intermittently revealed coils of barbed wire and the silhouettes of dogs. In the next was a selection of newspaper cartoons, of Franken in a Nazi SS uniform and of Charles Michel sweating over a school handwriting test while N-VA thugs threatened him with a cane. No one laughed; surrounding the cartoons, looking on at them, were enlarged photographs of eyes in stark, hooded faces, and towards the door a scarred arm and a turned, scarred back. In the final room the testimonies of asylum seekers held in Belgium's detention centres had been made into a collage written in red ink, and scraps of paper and cigarette packets lay on the floor for passers-by to pick up: names, phone numbers, a letter to a son. The title of the exhibition was *Dossier*; when I suggested to my friend that it might have been called *Nuance*, she first laughed, then covered her face with her hands and cried.

One Life: Sylvia Plath

Smithsonian National Portrait Gallery,
Washington D.C., 30 June 2017 – 20 May 2018

N. J. STALLARD

In spring 1954, Sylvia Plath dyed her hair from brunette to bleach blonde. Plath had recently returned to her studies at Smith College from her months at McLean Psychiatric Hospital. Marilyn Monroe had starred in *Gentlemen Prefer Blondes* the year before and blonde bombshells were in style. As a blonde, Plath went to New York to see some friends, art and plays, attended Harvard Summer School, wrote her first short story and had a poem published in *Harper's*. Then she dyed her hair back to brown.

To go blonde is always a symbolic gesture. A recent tweet by Jasmine Sha-Ree Sanders received 157k likes: 'I've learned that abruptly going from brunette to blonde (or vice versa!) is a white woman stress signal, kinda like when squid quickly change their colors, it's a sign of distress!' As well as a distress signal, bleach blonde hair can be a sign of emancipation, rebellion or an expression of boredom. It depends on the woman.

Plath's biographers tend to fixate on her brief stint as a blonde. The recent exhibition on Plath's life at the Smithsonian National Portrait Gallery, Washington DC, takes this fixation even further. The curators of the show, titled *One Life: Sylvia Plath*, aim to give the general public an alternative side to Plath's gloomy persona – the happy, sunny blonde to her serious, suicidal brunette.

'When she wanted to look more sensual and outgoing and vibrant she would have bright blonde hair,' explained Dorothy Moss, one of the exhibition's co-curators to Vogue. 'When she needed to look more intellectual and serious, to be taken seriously in her career, she would dye her hair back to brown.'

Reductive? There is evidence of Plath's opinion about hair colour in her letters. Further evidence is found in her 1955 short story 'Platinum Summer' about a roommate who dyes her hair blonde. However, this word 'evidence' is often used for Plath; both Janet Malcolm and Jacqueline Rose have written at length on how Plath's biography has become an endless whodunnit, in which biographers, estate handlers and readers can't help but mount a case in one direction or another.

The *One Life* exhibition suffers the same fate. Hair colour is taken as solid evidence of Plath's dualistic nature – she might have had one life, but she had two personalities. As the exhibition sells itself, in its own words: 'Visitors will get a look into Plath's personal life and her dualistic nature she explained as her "brown-haired" and "platinum" personalities.'

As a result, the exhibition is so myopic you begin to wonder if the curators were blinded by the ammonia. Located in a single small room of the Smithsonian, the selection of portraits and archival objects from Indiana University's Lily Library and Smith College are arranged in chronological order, beginning with one-year-old Plath in a 1933 family photo and ending with a clipping of Al Alvarez's epitaph in the *Observer*. The classic portraits are immediately familiar from various book jackets over the years: arm in arm with Ted Hughes on their wedding day or her curling brunette bangs in the classic author picture by Rollie McKenna. Alongside the portraits are artworks, letters, writing drafts and personal possessions, which range from artsy (Plath originally planned to major in studio art) and mundane (her girl scout uniform) to the Gothic (her severed childhood ponytail, kept by her mother, and her elm wood writing desk, made from the cut of a coffin lid by her brother).

Every opportunity is taken to point out Plath's dualist nature. A pair of paper dolls, handmade by Plath at the age of twelve, are not only proof of her 'keen interest in glamor' and early desire to become a fashion designer. 'For each doll, one brunette and one blonde, she created a wide array of fantastic and fashionable outfits with cinched waists and exaggerated cleavages,' reads the caption, to highlight a young mind's fascination with self-image and hair colour.

In the centre of the room, a glass vitrine contains a draft of her 1955 Senior Honors Thesis, titled 'The Magic Mirror: Study of the Double in Two of Dostoevsky's Novels', in which she 'compares and contrasts the split personalities in *The Double* and *The Brothers Karamazov*', cites Sigmund Freud and Otto Rank, and concludes: 'recognition of our various mirror images and reconciliation with them will save us from disintegration'.

The more vital piece of evidence is the two photographs of Plath from 1954, placed on the same stretch of wall at the focal point of the exhibition. The first photograph is titled by the curators as her 'Marilyn shot' – a photograph of Plath on the beach as a platinum blonde in a two-piece swimsuit, recently used for the cover of the UK edition of Faber's *Letters of Sylvia Plath: Volume I* (a choice which was described by Cathleen Allyn Conway in the *Guardian* as 'sexualised and frivolous'). The adjectives used in the caption of the Marilyn shot: daring, adventuresome, sultry, fashionable, beaming. The second photograph is titled 'Studio photograph of Sylvia Plath (with brown hair)'. Adjectives used in the caption: eager, serious, intellectual.

Monroe herself was a natural brunette, a compulsive reader and did not necessarily enjoy her rise to fame as the archetypal Hollywood dumb blonde. Interesting parallels can be made between Plath's and Monroe's place in the American imagination. However, none are made at *One Life*. Instead the comparison is offensive and solely reliant on clichés.

The chronological arrangement of the exhibition further traps Plath in her biography. The visitor is transformed into a detective, sifting through clues. Sticking to chronology feels like a missed opportunity to release an artist from the plot arc of her life and the troubled territory of her biography that so often distracts from her work.

Jacqueline Rose has emphasised the complex multiplicities found within Plath's oeuvre. Plath is a shape-shifter who experiments with her own self-image and the critic must be wary of any ambitions to 'try to construct a single, consistent image of Plath herself, not just because of the vested interests that so often appear to be at stake but because of the multiplicity of representations that Plath offers of herself'.

In *One Life*, this multiplicity is traded in for dualism and a bottle of bleach. It's a bad trade.

Letter from Wales

SAM ADAMS

I have written before, a long time ago, about driving south from Hay (Y Gelli) or thereabouts and, as the high-hedged country road dawdles this way and that, crossing and re-crossing the border: here we are in England and *Hurrah*, welcome again to Wales! There are so many Welsh names, of villages and farms, on the map of the Southern March to the east of Offa's Dyke – Pen-y-lan, Cayo, Cwmcoched, Bryngwyn, Marlas, Bagwyllydiart – extending as far as Hereford itself, that at fanciful moments I like to think the folk of south Herefordshire will one day vote themselves part of 'Greater Wales'. Though they have since moved to Abergavenny, for some years we regularly visited friends living in the village of Ewyas Harold and, thanks to them, became a little familiar with lanes and villages around and about. No one seems to know what 'Ewyas' means, beyond signifying the territory that still bears the name, but Harold is alleged to be the grandson of Æthelred the Unready. Approaching, within a mile of our friends' door we would pass through the hamlet of Llangua ('church of Ciwan', a female saint who lost the final 'n' of her name in the fifteenth century), take our turn at the lights commanding the bridge over the Monnow and enter England.

A few hundred yards farther brought us to Pontrilas ('bridge over the Dulas'), a Welsh name that superseded the English 'Heliston' as late as the eighteenth century, and soon after we turned sharp left into Ewyas Harold. If you traverse the village to follow another curving country lane for about five miles, doubling back westwards though still in England, you reach Clodock, a straggle of farms and cottages overlooked by Hatterrall Hill to the west and, in the topsy-turvy way of things hereabouts, Mynydd Merddin (Merlin's Mount) to the east. The parish is named after Saint Clydawg, a fifth-century martyr, a Celtic Saint. The site of his ancient shrine is now occupied by a remarkably well-preserved seventeenth-century church, which until 1852 was still in the diocese of St David's. The entire amalgam of local geography and history is expressive of border country. Fragments of painted wall are still visible inside the church and among its treasures is a ninth-century tombstone, discovered when the nave was excavated in 1917. The graveyard is full, crowded with hundreds of old headstones, but in an extension field across the road from the lychgate you will find the spot where Raymond Williams is interred. It is marked with a simple stone inscribed with only names and dates commemorating him and his wife, Joyce (known as Joy), also buried there. He would have appreciated the simplicity of marker and setting in this frontier zone, and ultimately his participation in the ineffable sense of continuity held in the green chalice of a rural parish.

So, in January 1988, the renowned social historian, cultural and political analyst, literary critic, novelist, came home, almost. He was born in Pandy, some three miles from Clodock and just over the border, in Wales. Why wasn't the circle neatly closed to bring him back to his beginnings? He and Joy had a cottage another half-dozen miles up the Monnow valley in Craswall, with Clodoch and Longtown one of a group of parishes set on the red soil of south Herefordshire, in the lee of the Black Mountains of east Wales, which supplied the sandstone for the construction of their homes and churches. In Pandy, his father, a World War One veteran, was a railway signalman and avid gardener-beekeeper who supplemented his income by selling produce at Hereford market. He was also an active member of the Labour Party. Raymond Williams attended the Henry VIII Grammar School in Abergavenny, and on the strength of Higher School Certificate results obtained a place at Trinity College, Cambridge, where he read English. His undergraduate studies were interrupted by the war, in which he served in an anti-tank regiment through the Normandy campaign to the fall of Germany. That done, he returned to full exposure with Leavisite practical criticism in Cambridge and complete his degree. Thereafter, a formative stint as staff tutor for the Oxford University Extra-Mural Delegacy, mostly in east Sussex, during which much of his thinking consolidated in *Culture and Society* (1958) was formulated, preceded his return to Cambridge as a lecturer (1961) and professor (1974).

In 1997, among the earliest of the finely crafted commemorative slate plaques put up by the Rhys Davies Trust was unveiled at his birthplace, a house named Llwyn Derw ('Oak Grove') just off the A465 Abergavenny–Hereford road. It is not immediately in the public gaze, but worth the trouble of asking directions. After the unveiling and a buffet lunch in a pub across the road, we dispersed well satisfied. The Trust had done its bit to underline that he was Welsh, one of us. But, of course, it isn't as simple as that. In an interview published in the *New Left Review* in 1979, he speaks of his boyhood, when Welsh was in a box, 'poems and songs... learnt by heart for special occasions', of his 'revulsion against what I saw as the extreme narrowness of Welsh Nonconformism', and the profound Anglicising influence of his grammar school education. With his long immersion in England, geographically and culturally, one would think all attachment to Wales would be severed beyond repair, but that was not the case. As he goes on to say, 'The result was a rejection of my Welshness which I did not work through until well into my thirties, when I began to read the history and understand it.'

In his novels, from *Border Country,* published in 1978 but begun many years earlier, to *People of the Black Mountains* (1989), character, setting, historical background, are consistently in borderland, but on the Welsh side. That creatively and imaginatively he remained in Wales is of no concern to the great majority of commentators who, while writing at length about his contribution as social historian, ignore his roots and his own acknowledgment of them. The work of Daniel Williams, *Who Speaks for Wales? Raymond Williams: Nature, Culture, Identity* (2003), and Dai Smith, his authorised biographer, *Raymond Williams: A Warrior's Tale* (2008), has asserted the opposing view, but it will bear reiterating. When the friend of whom I spoke in the opening paragraph visited Raymond Williams at his Craswall home in the 1970s to ask whether he would be interested in becoming a member of Yr Academi Gymreig, the Welsh academy of writers, without a moment's thought he said, 'Yes'.

Helen Dunmore

NEIL ASTLEY

First published on www.waterstones.com

I first met Helen in 1977 when I was working on *Stand* magazine, which had published a few of her poems. She came up to Newcastle to be interviewed for a vacant co-editor's post, and we took her on an outing to Holy Island as a way of getting to know her. Very wisely as it turned out (I left the magazine not long afterwards), she decided not to take the job, which would have involved moving up from Bristol. She'd recently returned from Finland, where she'd lived for two years after graduating from York University, and was wanting to devote as much time as possible to her writing: she would work as an office temp for two months, then reserve the next two months just for her writing; then earn enough from office work to spend another two months just writing. Some of her early poems and stories drew on her time in Finland as well as celebrating the lives of women. This was the period of the Greenham Common protests which Helen supported, and the first magazine to publish her work was *Spare Rib*.

We kept in touch, and when I set up Bloodaxe in 1978 I asked her if she'd send me the manuscript of her first collection once it was ready. This took a few years. She didn't want to rush the book. We had the core of a manuscript, and she sent me new poems as she wrote them. In the meantime, she had met and married her husband Frank Charnley, becoming a stepmother to his young son Ollie, and soon she had her own son, Patrick (followed much later by her daughter Tess). Family life and motherhood started to figure in the new work as the collection came together. When *The Apple Fall* was launched at Newcastle's Morden Tower in 1983, she had just turned thirty and was training to be a nursery teacher. Very few poetry collections by women were published at that time, and Helen's ability to combine the domestic with the universal – in poems remarkable for their rhythmical fluency and sensuousness – was an influence on other poets of her generation.

I wasn't surprised when she turned to fiction, her poetry being so strong in narrative, each poem telling its own story; and I was delighted to see how much her prose was illuminated by her beautiful use of language. Each novel was as much a pleasure to read as her poetry, and I loved savouring both. Despite her growing success as a novelist and children's writer, Helen continued to see her poetry as central to her writing. Every few years she'd set aside time to work on a new poetry collection, sending me a manuscript once she had accumulated thirty to forty poems she was happy with. Over the course of the next year, or sometimes longer, she'd send more poems, sometimes just one, other times two or three which were thematically linked. The collections were always completed like this, originally with single poems arriving by post, then later, one or two at a time, by email. It was lovely to keep in touch with her in this way. I never needed to give that much feedback to the poems, but whatever I did have to offer she always considered carefully.

With *Inside the Wave* the process was the same but the effect was alarmingly different. In April 2016 she delivered the initial manuscript, a smaller collection then entitled *Counting Backwards*, written while undergoing cancer treatment thought to have been successful. As with her just-written novel, *Birdcage Walk*, much of the work – but by no means all – related to mortality and death, to what and whom we leave behind. Over the next few months, eight more poems followed by email. Then in August she phoned with the devastating news that a previously undetected growth had been discovered – and too late. She'd been given less than a year to live, but she felt some consolation in having completed what would be her final novel and final poetry collection.

She continued to add new poems to the collection, using the Notes function on her iPhone to write from bed and then emailing them to me. The eight poems that completed the collection were among the most heartbreaking. 'My life's stem was cut' – the poem she wrote in response to her terminal diagnosis – brought tears to my eyes. Then she re-ordered the book to accommodate the last poems, commenting: 'It is exciting to see the collection typeset. It gives the poems that slight distance from me, as if they were ready to go out into the world. I'm so glad that you think the order works and that the poems reflect that sense of where the Underworld meets the human world.'

Inside the Wave achieved its power and greatness as a poetry collection largely because of how the manuscript was transformed in the course of Helen's final year, when a third of the poems – including some of those which readers have connected with most deeply – were added, not in chronological order, but placed where they strengthened the overall coherence of a book which is as much about celebrating life as facing death. She wanted the book to be read as an organically whole collection concerned with all areas of life and being.

A month after its publication, Helen told me she was 'living very quietly now during this last stage of my illness, cared for by Hospice at Home. They are fantastic.' And she sent me her final poem, 'Hold out your arms', written on her phone the day before, on 25 May 2017. The book had sold out in just a month, and she readily agreed to the poem being added to the first reprint, which we were able to make available shortly after her death last June.

I've often found that the best writers can be the least pushy and sometimes even the least confident of new work. I think that Helen always knew that she was a fine (I would say wonderful) poet, but she could still be quite tentative with new poems, not lacking in confidence but perhaps worrying that her absorption in her fiction was leaving the poetry out on a limb. Submitting 'The Malarkey' anonymously to the National Poetry Competition in 2010 achieved exactly what she was hoping for: validation from the poetry community in being judged by fellow poets who didn't know who'd written the winning poem.

She would have been both delighted and bemused had she known that *Inside the Wave* would win a Costa Book Award, something she never achieved with any of her brilliant novels, not even for *The Siege*, a magisterial book that was shortlisted for but unaccountably failed to pick up the Whitbread Novel Award in 2001. Yet readers – being read – mattered to her far more than prizes.

What she would have appreciated most about having *Inside the Wave* made Costa Book of the Year would be that so many of the people who loved her fiction would come to know her poetry as well. To borrow a comment she made about my anthology *Staying Alive*, it's 'a book for people who know they love poetry, and for people who think they don't'.

Letter from Washington

James Womack

I had been warned that DC was a city on the fritz, ragged around the edges, with a berserk president hiding in the storm drains dressed in a clown suit. This was not entirely true, but it was hard to get lost: you could measure your proximity to the White House by the number of people standing in the street and smoking. There was something in the air, and under the ground as well: a throb of power, maybe, but in whose hands was unclear. Despair on the cusp of becoming anger. Abandon. The idea that something had been lost. The best placard I saw in Lafayette Square read simply 'MAKE AMERICA AGAIN'.

I was there because of Turkmenistan. In 2002, around sixty people (the so-called 'Novembrists') were arrested in the Central Asian republic and accused of planning a coup against the president-for-life, Saparmurat Niyazov. One of the alleged Novembrists was Batyr Berdyev, a former foreign minister. He was arrested in December 2002, and the last reliable reports of him date back to 2005. In 2007, Niyazov's successor (and keen heir, and former dentist), Gurbanguly Berdymukhamedov, said that he thought Berdyev was still alive. Since then, nothing.

In 2003, Berdyev managed to smuggle a document out of prison. Not a manifesto, but a collection of thirty-six poems, addressed to his wife and infant son. We hope that Berdyev is still alive – he is a focus of the human rights campaign that aims to find out what has happened to the Turkmen disappeared (https://provetheyarealive.org) – but it is difficult to read the poems as anything other than a testament, a leave-taking. They are written from beyond a wall. Anyway, I co-translated the book; the book came out; I was invited to Washington to speak about it, and to engage in that kind of soft power that seems so unfashionable nowadays.

That's all background. I tell you, I was scared of the city, and nothing helped calm me. No reassurance in the supposed reassurances as I was lined up and processed through immigration. The Dignitas slogan of the concourse transit: *Welcome to Washington Dulles International Airport. We're here to help you along your way*. The advisory video on a painful loop as one hour at the border turned into two and then three: *Why are you taking mommy's fingerprints? Good question! To make sure someone isn't pretending to be your mom, and to keep you and your family safe*. Someone had lost a passenger and made regular calls for him over the intercom. *Peter Surreal, Peter Surreal? Could Peter Surreal please come to the information desk?* I told the man on the desk I was there for a few human rights meetings. *Human rights? I'm just going to have to take both sets of fingerprints, sir*.

The day was where the night should have been. Hotelled, I slept on a vast bed until three a.m., when I decided to walk to the Lincoln Memorial from where I was staying, in Alexandria, in a different state. I walked alongside the Potomac, through patches of odd creaking wildness, happy not to have thought in advance to google *Are there bears in DC?*. There were no bridges unvehicled humans were allowed to cross, so I kept on walking, the Washington Monument sparking red in the distance. I had to pass Arlington Cemetery before I found a permitted crossing, but I didn't think I had time to go and sit a while with the dead.

Even before most of the city was awake, there were still rubberneckers, wedding parties, ad campaigns crowded round the steps of the Lincoln Memorial. A woman in a sari, alongside her husband-to-be, having photos snapped at the feet of the vast statue. So white and secure of itself, with the seven a.m. sun upon it. I sat with the statue behind me and looked down the mall, sitting between others, mostly couples, doing the same thing. *It's a perfect photo fucking op*.

Later, we went to the State Department. As well as the organisers of the Turkmen campaign, a Kazakh journalist came as well, a representative of one of only three free newspapers in the country. A guy ahead of us in the queue to pass the scanner was allowed to bypass the beeping gate and sign his gun directly into the Weapons Log. Our contact led us through the hall of flags, and into an underground bunker. We passed the cafeteria. *If you have any questions or comments, write to cafeteriacomments@state.gov*. The room we went into, through three sets of security doors, still had the minutes of a previous meeting lying on the table. We looked away while they were shuffled into a cardboard folder.

Diplomacy, like dictatorship, is another one of the arts of euphemism. We were given generally positive answers to difficult questions, but no assurances – our contact could give us none. We were gently pressed for information we did not really have, that could help formulate a policy we did not know. Afterwards, the campaign organisers said that it had been a very good meeting, and described the lines I had to read between. Given the way we are being sold America at the moment, as the domain of a Falstaff with no irony or joy – an unscrupulous fat man scared of death – ambiguity was welcome, or at least refreshing.

At one of the other meetings we had during the week, I sat next to a woman who had 'Ask Tillerson' written in her notepad. Tillerson was euthanised four days after I got home. Behind all the monuments, power in the city seemed like something unruly. Meetings, meetings at which I was told that 'things had got done', seemed from the outside to be exercises in treading water, waiting for the current world to end. That night, when I got back to the hotel, I saw two white-stick blind men holding hands with a prostitute, which sounds like the punchline to a joke, but isn't.

Darning

BEVERLEY BIE BRAHIC

Roaming the library stacks makes me uneasy. Too many books I haven't read. The flesh is sad? Alas. But *I've read all the books*? Not even close. Getting my bearings in the third (literature) floor's musty pulp-and-paper-smelling undergrowth, I file down a narrow path between stacks to tip a few more books from the shelf.

My husband's sabbatical at a California university has stretched into years. I miss the street corner stink of piss, the damp zinc and glitter of life in Paris. I miss the newsstands. I miss the bookshops. The campus bookstore has been taken over by sportswear with the university logo; books relegated to the caves and eaves. In Paris, the flâneur is forever being lured into small shops still in business because French law restricts discounting and free shipping (no help, unfortunately, for Paris's English bookshops, like the much-regretted Village Voice, which must still compete with the online trade).

But the campus dweller life allows me to indulge an old fantasy: plugging the holes in my education. Sure, this feels like one of those math problems in which the student is asked to calculate how long it will take to fill a bathtub that is simultaneously draining at a different rate. Still I persist. A card swipe gets me into the university's Babelian library, its hushed reading rooms with rows of shiny new books (English spines one way, French the other) and the ferny canyon-like stacks. I can audit classes – heaven in my theology will be reading Dante's *Inferno* / Calvino's *Cosmicomics* in the dauntingly articulate company of students toting laptops on skateboards. I've screwed my courage to the sticking point for 'Philosophy and Literature', with readings from Aristotle to Lydia Davis's radically short story ('It has been so long since she used a metaphor!'): a course so rife with the stuff of thought that when I scrolled through the online catalogue recently and saw it was being offered again with what looked like a fresh slate of readings I messaged the teaching team – a Proust scholar and a historian of late modern philosophy – to beg permission to repeat. 'The good news,' my friend the philosopher shot back with characteristic Californian generosity, 'is that you are most welcome... the bad news is that the syllabus will be exactly the same. Even the jokes.'

I've never fathomed why the 'autodidact' in Sartre's *Nausea* was conceived as a comic figure. Was it a European thing: there are those born to education and the rest should lose their illusions and do something useful?

My useful task at the moment is translating a collection of poems by the French poet Yves Bonnefoy. In one poem a student sits late at night 'in an isolated house in the middle of a big garden' reading Augustine. Nodding off, he dreams he is back in his childhood room, where trains would rumble past the bottom of the garden in the middle of the night. Suddenly – is he dreaming? is he awake? – he is startled by the sound of a pebble tossed against the window; stepping outside he finds a ragged old woman he's seen before, but can't place. 'He knows he has already taken those thin hands / in his, on a table.'

The poem's late night fireside setting brings Coleridge to mind; searching for the words to make Bonnefoy's poem shimmer to life in English I raid 'Frost at Midnight'. I like dipping into Coleridge, Wordsworth and Yeats for words and images to help translate Bonnefoy who has himself translated into French English poets from Shakespeare to Yeats – bringing writers together across time and languages is one of translation's particular delights. But the importance of the old woman in the poem and her connection to Augustine, if connection there is, remain mysterious to me. The words in their dictionary dress are familiar, but my translation feels thin, lacking in the visceral understanding that comes when one's experience and the poet's find a common ground. Perhaps the philosophical concepts underpinning the poem elude me? My knowledge of philosophy is spotty.

Perusing the university course catalogue I discover, what luck, that the Classics Department is offering a seminar on Augustine, and I am welcome to sit in. I request the reading list. Whether it will help me translate Bonnefoy's poem is unclear, what I do know is that I relish spending an afternoon a week reading Augustine under the tutelage of a specialist.

The class also shows me how thin my knowledge of history is. One evening, reading a biography of Augustine, distracted by the squirrels racing effortlessly up and down redwood trees, I light on the words 'Sack of Rome' – an event of which I have only the vaguest notions. Reluctantly – so many books wait to be read! – I set the *Confessions* aside and take time to gather some moss on the internet. Rome, it turns out, was sacked not just once (Berlusconi rates a mention on Wikipedia's 'disambiguation' page); in Augustine's day it sent boatloads of Romans fleeing to North Africa. Mass slaughter, refugees... 'The lamb?' asks Bonnefoy in a poem, 'Only ever / the knife and the blood'. Here, at least, is some familiar ground.

An hour slips past. Two. Finally, I retrace my footsteps, linger at the Visigoths who sacked Rome on the 24 August AD 410 – what precision! ('The barbarians are coming today', Cavafy wrote). Reading about the death and burial of Alaric, the Visigoth leader, makes me wish I knew more about Alaric.

Everything leads to something else. I am not advancing my quest to understand Bonnefoy's poem. Or perhaps I am. This kind of amplification and qualification explains how Tristram Shandy took so long to be born. How Leibniz, writing the history of the House of Brunswick, tunnelled deeper and deeper, angering his patrons who only wanted a fairytale... how Proust burrows into his childhood and resurfaces a lifetime later. 'A dizzying net of divergent, convergent and parallel times' (Borges, *The Garden of Forking Paths*).

Bonnefoy's poem and Augustine recede. In their place, in a cobwebby corner of my mind, I see our long dead neighbour in the south of France. She lived with her unmarried son, our friend P––, in the farmhouse that adjoins my husband's family's ancestral homestead. In the evening we'd find her in the kitchen, the hearth over which she had cooked still glowing. She'd be darning. She was proud of her handiwork – thick work socks that were more darn than sock. Now her small bent body, that I never saw out of mourning, diminishes up the stairs. Tomorrow she'll get on with her darning. I close my computer. Tomorrow I'll have another go at the holes in my education. And Bonnefoy's poem.

from The Notebooks of Arcangelo Riffis

MARIUS KOCIEJOWSKI

My friend, several months before he died, asked if he could request a favour of me and, mindful of the extraordinary demands he made from time to time, I said it depended on what that favour was. 'When I die,' he whispered, 'I want you to plunge a dagger into my heart.' It would have to be a dagger, of course, a *poetical* blade, and not an ordinary serrated kitchen knife. This once most physically strong of men slowly moved his weakly clenched fist to his chest three times in a stabbing motion. There was some particular awfulness in his eyes. 'I don't want to be buried alive,' he murmured. I waited a little. I waited a bit more. 'Why are you depriving me,' I asked him, 'of the pleasure of doing it *now*?' Arcangelo Riffis smiled the flicker of a smile he often made when caught between resignation and sheer exasperation with me.

*

At seven in the morning, 6 March 2008, just two days after his sixty-eighth birthday, I knelt on the floor over his still-warm body, an ungainly heap of flesh and bone, more bone than flesh, the contents of his ashtray spilled about him. Other matters connected to that scene I won't go into here. We may rid the brain of certain things by speaking of them, so say our guides to emotional welfare, but it's not always the healthy exercise they say it is. Arcangelo's eyes were still open, fixed upon nothing in particular yet carrying within them the desperate petitioning of a few months before. Where was that kitchen implement with the serrated edge, the black handle?

Three things only I had to get out of his room for fear something might happen to them in his absence: the 1952 Oxford University Press edition of Shelley's *Poetical Works*, Arcangelo's notebooks, fifty in all, and the silver Parker ballpoint pen with which he wrote, always in blue ink, every single word that went into them. I must take care of his precious pen, he told me, which he'd owned since the age of thirteen, which he bought at a reduction because, a manufacturer's fluke, the clasp on it was put on backwards. Over the years it had come to assume a talismanic value in his eyes. All the women he ever loved, he told me, held that pen at least once and it was with it that he wrote his *carmina*. If poetry was this quixotic knight errant's shield, he'd say, that pen was his lance. The volume of Shelley was that with which he courted his first, perhaps his only, true love. The notebooks became mine by default, there being nobody else for them to go to, and, besides, he had already said to me I'd be surprised by some of the things I'd find in them after he'd gone. Yes, I would be, I was, I *am*. They've become the character with whom I now wrestle. The notebooks of Arcangelo Riffis, all fifty of them, sit on the shelf behind me as I write, the majority of them Prussian blue, *his* colour, narrow feint, nine by seven inches, smelling of cigarette smoke. I have begun to regret the gradual disappearance of that smell as if soul were somehow inextricable from it. When I visited him every Sunday afternoon, from one to three-thirty p.m. precisely, it was all I could do not to choke in that visibly white atmosphere, so thick sometimes I'd ask him to open the window a little. One day he sprayed air conditioner, claiming it would displace the smoke, atom for atom, and, of course, all it did was to perfume the choking haze. I asked him who he thought he was kidding. Yet now I'll raise one of those notebooks to my nose, thinking, with regret, one day the smell of tobacco will be completely gone. *All will be gone, all we ever were will cease to be.*

The narrow feint notebooks predeceased him. When they were no longer produced it almost drove him and, by extension, me, to distraction. Confined to his room for the better part of two decades, he pleaded with me to find him more of those notebooks. They had to be Prussian blue, narrow feint, nine by seven inches, but, try as I did, in a world gone metric, a world already close to done with paper, a world shot through with obsolescence, I'd come back empty handed, and then desperation would fill his eyes, as if enough of it would bring those precious notebooks back into existence.

'What can I do,' I protested, 'they're not being made anymore.'

'But there must be some *somewhere*,' he pleaded.

Any time I went abroad I was to search for narrow feint notebooks. Ottawa, Rome, Damascus. Damascus, I was to look there of all places. (Damascus, old stomping ground for my enquiries into human nature, what would Arcangelo say to the news from there?) I did come close one time, acquiring through an American contact ten clothbound notebooks that were narrow feint but not as wide, nine by six inches, and they were of a sandy colour, not his manly Prussian blue. They would not do, he argued, they would not accommodate his prose style. The dimensions of those earlier notebooks, he explained, took on perfectly the measure and rhythm of his thought. And then, curled up on the bed that misfortune had made the greater part of his domicile, he gave me a demonstration, not with the Parker ballpoint in his hand but rather *as if* he were holding it, which made me think *what a pain in the neck you are*, and as he reached the end of his invisible line of prose his hand went off the edge of the page and onto the bed. *Come now!* I guffawed. 'The pen is balanced in such a way,' he wrote in one of his Prussian blue narrow feint notebooks, 'so that the cartridge treads the paper with a gentle steadfast sound, letting the night and silence itself know you are stirring there. It has always been that way with old pens, from the goose quill to the nib, whereas a typewriter profanes silence, shunts and rattles, jars against the night. I've often wondered if the decline of the lyric and nuance in modern writing has anything to do with that unlovely, mechanistic noise.' He was nothing if not particular and so he went on to describe, yet again, and in precisely the same words he'd employed so many times before, the physical properties required of his notebooks. *Yes*, I muttered, *yes, yes, yes*.

'So you won't even give them a chance,' I cried, seizing back the sandy-coloured notebooks that are now on my shelves. I felt growing inside me a small dust devil of annoyance that without much further ado would become a cyclone of rage. *All I want is to enter my House justified.* I was ready to blow up his metaphorical house. And yet deep down I knew he'd persuaded me. We really do need that which accommodates our style. A couple of months later, I found red notebooks, wrong colour, of course, but of the desired height and width and thickness. They were not narrow feint, not quite, just a tiny bit too much space between the ruled lines. Again these would not do and it was then I abandoned the search. When I suggested he learn to adapt a bit more, Arcangelo glowered at me. Certain things were sacrosanct or, to use his phrase, *in the realm of the sacramento*. So it was with everything. When, in his final months, he moved from the dark and miserable room he had occupied for close to two decades into one where the light fell in heaps through a big window he bemoaned the absence of the trapezoid of dusty sunlight that at a certain hour fell across the foot of his bed in the ill-lit room where previously he wrote, when quickly he'd get the words down onto the page before the patch of light moved on. Now there was *too much* light.

'Well, draw the curtains then!'

Arcangelo did not like curtains. Maybe they were overly imbued with significance. And then there was the want of birdsong. Truly it was inexplicable. Why, although the place into which I moved him could not have been more than a quarter of a mile away from where he lived previously, were there trees outside and no birds in them? I looked down into the rectangle of gardens, hemmed in by the surrounding houses, and saw not even a flicker in the branches. This seemed to him a deathly omen of some kind and I who place great store in birds as harbingers of both good and evil could not but silently agree with him. 'The sedge has wither'd from the lake, / And no birds sing.' (Strangely we hardly ever spoke of Coleridge.)

So then, those narrow feint notebooks, the moving patch of sunlight, birdsong: there was never a man more specific in his needs, which, though few, were not extravagant for he was a man who lived on very little, who wanted for very little, and for those very few things to be taken away from him it was as if the very supports of his existence, all that had ensured the strict conditions of his several degrees of existence, were being kicked away from under him one by one. When finally they were gone then surely he, too, would have to take his leave. I took the Shelley, the pen with the inverted clasp, and the notebooks home.

*

A preliminary glimpse at the notebooks took me directly to the bitterest pages of our relationship. Why *there*? Why, from out of a total of fifty notebooks, did I have to open *that* particular one only to have ripped from my memory its many layers of soiled bandages? I almost reeled from the savagery with which he attacked me. It wouldn't have been so bad had his aim been true, I might have felt deserving of it, but the fact I had become for him, at that early stage in our relationship, the embodiment of all that he most hated in the world, the world as it had become for him – Swift's Laputa, its deity 'the whore reason' – made it difficult for me to read those passages with equanimity. Surely he knew me better than to lay those charges. But I must begin at the beginning where at the head of the first page of the first notebook he writes what surely, for him, were the most ironic of words – *Deus nobis haec otia fecit*:

Bruxelles, February 26, 1969, 7.42 a.m. Drizzly. Pitched four notebooks into the Tiber before leaving Rome for Genoa – a twitchy, spasmodic sort of *Italian Journal*, & three sheaves of London scribbling – in one of which must have been enfolded the jealously guarded poetic fragments culled from Chelsea. This has happened three times since… the *Hejira*. These last three days have been a sombre parody of what happened in 'Frisco in the first week of April 1966 – a wild search for blue-markings, rummaging through clothes & papers, fitful leafings through books, over & over, and two days of black despair & bitter cat-sleep.

England again within two months – Kensington this time, Earls Court. I shall seek permanent residence. That sad, outraged, mutilated & betrayed land, contemporary England is such a dismal place for an Anglophile – I dread to think what it must be like for a patriotic Englishman with its duckling of Bedford – I'd prefer the career of Sigismundo Malatesta to the britling duck's obscene antics a thousand times over – and its matriarchy of a parliament rattling & shambling to the leers & grimaces of that obscene little stumblebum Wilson. There is no more cheaply sordid, weakly vicious, thoroughly rotten type of degenerate humanity than that which is met with quite frequently there. I could call forth a roll of outstanding public examples & relate personal experiences that would go on for pages but it's too, too bloody depressing. Great Britain, once the proudest, mightiest, freest realm the world has ever seen, has become Mr Wilson's flea circus. God grant I'll be there when that smelly little rotter sinks, blinking, back into the mire from which *it* crawled. The present situation there is certainly unprecedented & a throwback to nothing in her history. But what is there on the horizon? *Mr Heath*? A colourless crustacean if there ever was one.

London *swings*, to be sure, to the rafters, by both wrists, like one of de Sade's females, *brutalised silly*, giggling, whimpering, simpering, whining, howling with mirthless hilarity under the lash. Harold ('over to you') Macmillan's bathetic, blubbering oration over the body of 'Bobby' Kennedy, pouring relentless libations of saccharined mucus into the microphone. (I became literally *queasy*.) Imagine what Dryden, Swift, Pope, Walpole or Lord Byron would make of the scene, Macmillan blowing through his moustache to the effect that 'Britain has *been* great, *is* great, and will *continue* to be great.' A more ludicrous performance could scarcely be imagined. Macmillan seemed, in his very person, to embody the national decay he supposed himself to be confuting. He exuded a flavour of mothballs. His decomposing visage & somehow seedy attire conveyed the impression of an aging & eccentric clergyman who had been induced to play the part of prime minister in the dramatized version of a C. P. Snow novel put on by a village amateur dramatic society. He goes on for four more hilarious paragraphs in this vein, in the finest, most classic, tradition of British wit but then suddenly fizzles out in blustering incoherence as the best of things British tend to do these days.

A Few More Offhand Remarks About More Than One Overwhelming Literary Giant

FRANK KUPPNER

1. A superb fluency and fluidity of image-making carries him off again and again into areas which he himself gets completely lost in. But it never seems to impair the dazzling confidence in his tone of voice.
2. Yes. If the image is dazzling enough, it will seem to prove any even half-plausible contention or argument that it is attached to. And who can take a proper, closer more critical look while *dazzled*?
3. But how much value can there possibly be in the elaboration – be it never so subtly, vividly and brilliantly done – of a view which, in its basic fabric, is quite massively delusional?
4. Truly, my darling – if delusion were to be made illegal, what an unimaginably vast amount could legitimately be accumulated in fines!
5. But evidently Reality is merely the wrapping-paper round the actual gift.
6. We can only hope that the dazzling brilliance of an image does not itself guarantee its fundamental *in*accuracy either!
7. Yes. A single fly out of so many possible. Nonetheless – a fly lands on the Great Pyramid and almost at once start laughing. Indeed. Don't we all know the feeling?
8. God creates infinite distances because he so greatly wishes to overcome precisely those same infinite distances.
9. No, Ada. Nothing we ever say or do – absolutely nothing – has any sort of likeness or similitude to Eternity. (And, if I may so put it, *even less* to Infinity.)
10. Unintelligible remarks from a source utterly unknowable by us!
11. But it is worth remembering all the same that to be so obsessed by one's own insignificance is itself a form of delusion of grandeur.
12. No. The genuine religious artist or thinker runs up and down and in and out and through the sacred places, shouting: 'Please! Don't look at *me*, whatever else you do! No. I'm perfectly serious!'
13. Such vast expenditures of time and energy, dedicated to communicating (often so wonderfully successfully!) with the totally non-existent! [What? Are there *degrees* of non-existence?]
14. For it would seem we are never nearer to touching on the Absolute directly than when we talk absolute nonsense. (Those, at least, who first of all have really, deeply thought about the matter. Meditated on it *profoundly*. And of course always providing we do so with a suitably humble awareness of our own absolute and inescapable limitations, Quin.)
15. Self-evidently, it will be no easy task to tie down the non-Existent to any one specific location.
16. Besides which, I myself am evidently a quite different somebody else from the somebody else I naively thought I was.
17. It is sometimes, my Lord, as if we were all merely the understudies, is it not? Just going through the motions. Yes. Not really the right people for the role. (Except, of course, for the uniquely blessed and self-sustaining loved one, if any.) But how are we to be blamed for this? At the very least, we didn't arrange the casting, did we? (All extras in an infinite crowd scene who think they are [or ought to be?] Hamlet. (At least!))
18. Evidently the Universe is perfectly happy to accept counterfeit money. Yes. Look, for instance, at all these crazily anti-realistic creeds; all these lethally over-simple political templates – which think they can talk about absolutely everything using, as it were, not much more than the dream of a vague tickle at the back of the throat.
19. Fortunately, only I am not affected by the trivial mental systems so uniquely characteristic of the present generation.
20. But might one not reasonably have expected the Author to have noticed that the protagonists of his tales are almost invariably moral idiots? This must surely lessen their effectiveness. Who are the tales treating of? To whom do they apply? What idiot is going to read them – and then have the insight to realise: 'Yes! I am precisely that cretin! Well spotted, Maestro!'
21. Truly, these men have been very badly served by the relentless intuitive accuracy of their faithful misinterpreters and mistranslators!
22. How else is one to put it? This very possibly quite sane and cultured gentleman is able to accept, however strugglingly, that an extremely variable anthology of aged Sinitic – no, no: sorry – *Semitic* literature somehow or other really did descend from a [metaphorical?] divine publishing-house somewhere [metaphorically?] beyond those actual stars. (Of course, there is no question of a mere *mechanism* here.)
23. Yes, Eve. A progressive or advanced theological thinker is, by and large, someone who is occasionally prepared to talk, though perhaps only to outsiders, as if there were at least some sort of theoretical possibility that his own preferred anti-realistic fantasy were somehow, to some extent at least, not the absolutely *whole* truth of the matter. (Present company excepted, of course. After all, if it's no use to you, why not just ignore it?)
24. The question of how one gains or can gain an impression of the Transcendent is very easily answered. One doesn't. One can't. After all – assuming such a thing does actually exist – it's transcendent. (What? Or *isn't* it?)
25. And all that could honestly be said of 'the Unchanging' is that it is unchanging. (Not that there could actually ever be anybody there to say it – or, indeed, do anything else – under any such utterly static circumstances.)
26. For to be 'eternally changing' and yet alive is, in any realistic sense, impossible. A mere contradiction in terms. Life is necessarily a process and therefore involves change. That is what any real process actually *is*. A change. A from X–Y.
27. Any real thing, any alteration of anything anywhere – any act, thought, decision, utterance, change of mind (or, for that matter, any resolution to stay the same) – utterly annihilates Timelessness.
28. Yes, darling. I too had a moment of precise intuition that something rather like that must be something fairly close to being the case. So. Let's change the subject to something merely real, shall we?

In Praise of the Fat Black Woman & Volume

KEI MILLER

I

THERE IS A POEM from *The Cartographer Tries to Map a Way to Zion* that I almost never read in England. There is something of the volume of that poem which seems out of place – even crude – in the supposed quiet of a British landscape. It is poem xxiii, in which the Rastaman chants most loudly, calling for the fall of Babylon – a proper nyabinghi chant, a summoning of fire and brimstone. The first time I read that poem in public was in Trinidad. I really was in no state to give a reading that night. Thirty hours earlier, I had been in the Middle East – in Northern Iraq, giving poetry workshops in the shadow of bombed-out buildings. I had flown a torturous route – Iraq to Vienna, Vienna to London, then London to Trinidad. My body was confused by all the climate changes – starting from the dry desert, going through the last strains of a European winter, and deposited at last into the tropical heat of the Caribbean. I should have gone straight to sleep, but instead they drove me from the airport to the reading venue. I am not certain now why I chose to read that particular bit of verse; perhaps it was an instinctive knowing that some poems have within them their own energy and need little help from their readers. Still it surprised me how, given voice, the poem was such a different animal from how it sat tamely on the page. It wasn't the poem's own volume that surprised me, but how it in turn elicited volume. It seemed to ask for a chorus of chanters and the Caribbean crowd willingly provided this. Lighters were lit up against the night, hands were clapping and someone shouted that most militant Rastafari shout: *More Fire!*

I knew such a poem would not work the same way in England. It could not. So I have mostly left it alone to do its quieter work on the page. Some sounds are not easily accommodated in a British landscape. Some sounds do not make sense here. A passage from Ishiguro's *Remains of the Day* has always stayed with me, and is instructive. It is that moment when Mr Stevens, the butler, is pondering the supposed greatness of Great Britain:

> And yet what precisely is this 'greatness'? Just where, or in what, does it lie? I am quite aware that it would take a far wiser head than mine to answer such a question, but if I were forced to hazard a guess, I would say that it is the very lack of obvious drama or spectacle that sets the beauty of our land apart. What is pertinent is the calmness of that beauty, its sense of restraint. It is as though the land knows of its own beauty, of its own greatness, and feels no need to shout it. In comparison, the sorts of sights offered in such places as Africa and America, though undoubtedly very exciting, would, I am sure, strike the objective viewer as inferior on account of their unseemly demonstrativeness.

Perhaps this is it. Perhaps I do not read the poem because of what I fear will be seen as its 'unseemly demonstrativeness'. Still, there are days when I think if anyone were to read that poem, and in this landscape, and not only to read it, but to solicit from the timid audience a chant of 'More Fire' or 'Jah! Rastafari!' it would be the Fat Black Woman. I have loved her for so many years, from the time I met her in Jamaica and she began to tell me many things – about poetry, about theory and about this other country that I would be moving to, and how I might fight for a space within it.

*

My early encounters with England and with Englishness had been through literature. There were, of course, many Englands that I met on the page, for here was a literature so old and so vital that the country stretched itself across time and locations and dialects. From the valiant campaigns of knights to the courtly world of kings, from the balls and dinners of Jane Austen to the bleakness of Charles Dickens, and all the way up to a post-war country, the complexion of its cities radically changing as its colonial subjects poured in to help rebuild. It was here, on the page, that I met the Fat Black Woman.

Grace Nichols's 1982 collection – the *Fat Black Woman's Poems* – is, ironically, a slim collection, and Grace Nichols a slim woman. And yet, I had always imagined the Fat Black Woman as her own author. It is in fact Nichols who encourages us to do this in the very title of the collection – that possessive which grants the character authorship. The Fat Black Woman will not only be written about but will share in the writing of herself. The Fat Black Woman defies our expectations; she rejects the stereotypes that have been thrown at her like ill-fitting hand-me-downs that she should still be grateful to wear. She is not some big breasted, head-rag wearing mammy figure. She is no Aunt Jemima flipping pancakes for the pickaninnies. Such roles would deny her her sexuality or a certain sophistication. At best, such roles allow her a kind of folksy wisdom, but never intellect or theoretical complexity. The Fat Black Woman, however, glories in her sexuality, the pleasure of her own soft centre, and also she relishes her mind – the sheer playfulness of her thoughts, and how she is able to bring strange and sometimes dissonant ideas into a productive relationship with each other.

Despite her strong sense of self and her humorous outlook, it is not always easy for the Fat Black Woman. She knows herself, but England hardly knows her at all. Sometimes she attempts to speak to the world, but her sounds do not always make sense in the cold landscape. Oftentimes she is shooshed, or not heard, or miraculously, not seen.

The Fat Black Woman lives in a world whose 'Everyman' – that suspicious hero who has since migrated from literature to Hollywood and so still stands today as the standard bearer of 'the universal story' – is almost always slim, white and male. In class, my students often tell me that they would like to write a 'universal story' and I think they have the advantage to do this because they are white, and from England, and almost any story they write with characters who look like them will be considered universal. But Grace Nichols's character and co-author, triply othered – fat and black and female – stands as Everyman's antithesis. She is a person whose stories are only ever specific to her – a person whose stories will only ever be 'black' stories, or 'woman' stories. The Fat Black Woman is systematically denied the broader representative powers which she sometimes yearns for. In one of her poems she watches the Miss World pageant, hopeful and despondent at the same time:

> Tonight the fat black woman
> is all agaze
> Will some Miss (Plump at least
> If not fat and black) uphold her name
>
> The fat black woman awaits in vain
> Slim after slim aspirant appears
> Baring her treasures in hopeful despair

The poem is poignant precisely for the way it holds the two contrasting emotions in close proximity – the hope, and the despair. Rather than negate, they accentuate each other. The Fat Black Woman cannot help but hope that she could live in a world – in an England – that accommodates her, but isn't so naïve to think it would ever happen. In watching the Miss World Pageant, the Fat Black Woman once again encounters a world of aesthetics that cannot see beauty in her own body.

In 'The Embodiment of Disobedience: Fat Black Women's Unruly Political Bodies' Andrea Shaw writes:

> Fatness and blackness have come to share a remarkably similar and complex relationship with the female body: both characteristics require degrees of erasure in order to render women viable entities by Western Aesthetic standards. Beauty pageants attest to this erasure: the more a contestant's body conforms to the cultural ideal of slenderness and the better a contestant can 'perform' whiteness both physiologically and behaviourally, the more improved her chances at success.

The Grace Nichols poem that I keep returning to is 'Tropical Death'. In it, the Fat Black Woman expresses perhaps a morbid nostalgia for the funereal rituals of the Caribbean. She desires to be the author not just of poems, but of her own death, or at least the rituals that will inevitably surround her dying. There are sounds that often attend death in the Caribbean – loud sounds – and to her own ears, these sounds are beautiful. These beautiful and loud sounds, however, do not make sense in England. The restrained and quiet landscape cannot make sense of such volume:

> The fat black woman want
> A brilliant tropical death
> Not a cold sojourn
> In some North Europe far / forlorn
>
> The fat black woman want
> some heat / hibiscus at her feet
> blue sea dress
> to wrap her neat
>
> The fat black woman want
> some bawl
> no quiet jerk tear wiping
> a polite hearse withdrawal
>
> The fat black woman want
> All her dead rights
> First night
> Third night
> Nine night
> All the sleepless droning
> Red eyed wake nights
>
> In the heart
> of her mother's sweetrest
> in the shade
> of the sunleaf's cool bless
> in the bloom
> of her people's bloodrest
>
> the fat black woman want
> a brilliant tropical death yes.

When Fiona Sampson quotes this poem in her book 'After the Lyric', she redacts the two stanzas that stand out to me, the third and fourth, from 'The fat black woman want / some bawl' to 'All the sleepless droning / red eyed wake nights'. It was here that I began to think of more than what Andrea Shaw calls the Fat Black Woman's disobedient and unruly political body – but also her aesthetics, her poetics. The Fat Black Woman, already triply othered, is in fact a site of multiple alterities. It is not just her weight, her race and her gender that sets her apart from everyman but also her sense of what is beautiful – her desire for volume – and her ability to read complexity, sophistication and perfectly pitched tastefulness within that volume. The Fat Black Woman would like to hear a good old-fashioned bawl – a screaming out – and then to be lulled by those sleepless droning red-eyed wake nights. But all of this is unavailable to her in the politeness of Britain.

I must be fair to Samson. In 'After The Lyric' she is not anthologising Nichols but writing about her critically; she can only reference parts of the poem. Still, it is interesting to me that it is these particular lines – this call for volume – that is inadvertently muted.

The Fat Black Woman when weighed beside and against the slim white everyman, embodies not only disobedience and unruliness but a necessary corrective, a sort of counter-aesthetic, a necessary rejection of the ways we have tended to valorise restraint and subtlety as markers of poetic excellence. The Fat Black Woman privileges excess – though even this word 'excess' might be problematic for the Fat Black Woman. It suggests, perhaps, that a committee somewhere decided on what would be considered sufficient quantity. But who was on this committee? When and where did they meet? How did they make their decisions? Which cultures, which counter ideas of beauty and wit, which alternative exercises of intelligence are (purposely or inadvertently) excluded from its small remit?

II

The Fat Black Woman has pushed me into difficult waters – waters that I am ill equipped to swim in. Here in the present ocean of this essay are massive philosophical ideas about aesthetics and the appreciation of art – ideas that have carried on from Aristotle to Hegel to Kant, back and forth questions of whether beauty is inherent or socially constructed, on whether aesthetics as a discipline belongs to the sciences or to philosophy? What does it mean to be a human in search of beauty? What does it mean to work as an artist involved in the construction of beauty?

I choose to paddle in a slightly smaller pond. My concern here is poetry, and its critical reception, especially here in England. I want to challenge that old and unrelenting aesthetic that has tried (whether knowingly or not) to set limits on the volume at which good poetry can be pitched.

This is a debate that has always split me with surprising neatness. On the one hand, the critic in me accepts that ideas of beauty, cultures of aesthetics are socially constructed. I am wholly persuaded by Simon Gikandi's argument that the Western culture of aesthetics was profoundly affected by the institution of slavery. 'Slavery and taste,' he writes 'came to be intimately connected even when they were structurally constructed as radical opposites.' He is therefore interested in the 'introjection of slavery into the realm of manners, civility, sense and sensibility'. Ideals that we still hold in such esteem today – ideas of restraint and subtlety and quiet, were in fact counterpoints to the perception of the enslaved black body. It was bodies such as the Fat Black Woman's, and bodies such as my own, and a perception of the cultures from which these bodies had been stolen that became useful opposites with which to define and construct a new modernity. To be civilised, to be mannered, to be a person of good taste was to be as different from the Fat Black Woman as possible.

The critic in me is saddened by the profound damage and erasures that these ideas of civility and beauty have done to us – the fact of black women who might never see themselves as beautiful, or the fact that the boyishly handsome dancehall artist from Jamaica, Beenie Man, can sing with such pride 'Mi black and mi ugly, a Africa mi come from'. Or the fact that Caribbean people who want sometimes to bawl, must try to contain themselves, or else feel uncivilised and uncouth to give in to that counter aesthetic.

Sometimes the critic in me feels that this whole business of aesthetics has been so deeply hurtful that we should do away with it completely, if only to stop those ripples that have never stopped spreading since the stone of chattel slavery was dropped into the waters of our collective humanity.

But how could I ever do away with aesthetics – the whole beautiful shebang of it, however distasteful its undersides? I am not only a critic; I am primarily a writer – a poet and a novelist. I am someone whose daily work tries to create beauty rather than dismantle the flawed systems by which we appreciate such beauty. Some days – I do not mind admitting this – I think of myself as an ambitious writer. I would like the book I write today to be better than the book I wrote yesterday. With such ambition comes the necessary acceptance of goal posts. What do I mark as good, and what then is better? I also teach Creative Writing, and if I am to tell a student that this poem or this passage doesn't work, or that this sentence is muddled or clunky, or that this line could be better, then once again I must accept and buy into a culture of taste, perhaps even the very culture of taste that my critical self would like to rebel against.

I live therefore in a deeply conflicted state, recognising that I have been able to flourish artistically within a system that was constructed to exclude me, and my body, and the sounds that come out of black mouths. It is a system that continues to exclude several of my peers whose poems might be deemed too loud or too aggressive. I make a compromise. It is not ideal. It could never be ideal. Perhaps at heart, I am an incrementalist. I try to write poems that gradually turn up the volume. I want to adjust my readers' ears, slowly, slowly, to a world of sound and beauty that they had not been capable of hearing before.

It is work that must be done. Of critical importance here is our profound impoverishment because of the vast continents of poetry that we have either dismissed too casually or never heard at all because it came to us like ultrasound – pitched at volumes so loud the English ear was unable to hear them. Of critical importance here is the critical language which we continue to use in reviewing discourse, words we offer up in our assessment of whether a poem or a collection is good or bad, words that pretend to be neutral but are burdened with so much history – words that I have hinted at before like subtle, quiet, restrained, elegant. These are words that have been attached to my own work but which I suggest act as a sort of dog whistle criticism. The majority of people might not hear what is happening beneath such accolades, not even those who genuinely meant to compliment me, but to some extent I am being praised for the extent to which I am black, but not too black – the ways in which I have pitched blackness at an appropriate volume. Of critical importance here, as our cities and writing cultures become so much more diverse and cross-pollinated, is the extent to which such an outdated sense of taste unfairly disadvantages both black and white poets who don't perform beauty or intelligence in expected ways, and on the other unfairly privileges both white and black poets who know how conform to these norms.

III

I will probably be fairly accused of indulging in an overly Romantic and folksy essentialising of what it means to be from the Caribbean and to write the Caribbean, but sometimes I think every Caribbean poet is really a Fat Black Woman – or at least we all have Fat Black Woman tendencies. Even Walcott did – he who was so often seen as the most English of us, the Caribbean poet most comfortable to embrace Western tradition. 'I feel no shame in having endured the colonial experience,' he once wrote. 'It was cruel, but it created our literature.' Over and over Walcott has articulated similar thoughts – counting himself not just as any inheritor but a royal inheritor into the tradition of English language poetry. 'The English language is nobody's special property. It is the property of the imagination; it is the property of the language itself. I have never felt inhibited in trying to write as well as the greatest English poets.' But that tradition could seem so quiet, that the Fat Black Woman did not rush into it. Walcott was aware of her absence, even as he accused her unfairly of not writing as well as she could. 'I yearn for the company of better Caribbean poetry, quite frankly. I feel a little lonely.'

Too much has been made about the supposed lines drawn between the two great Caribbean poets, Derek Walcott and Kamau Brathwaite. We like to imagine them constantly side-eyeing each other. But this much is fair, that Brathwaite has been the poet-critic much more invested in challenging the very culture of taste and aesthetics that favoured poets such as Walcott. Whereas Walcott writes, 'My life must not be made public / until I've learned to suffer in accurate iambics', Brathwaite famously writes:

> What is even more important as we develop this business of emergent language in the Caribbean, is the actual rhythm and the syllables, the very software, in a way, of the language. What English has given us as a model for poetry, and to a lesser extent prose (but poetry is the basic tool here), is the pentameter... But the pentameter carries with it a certain kind of experience, which is not the experience of the hurricane. The hurricane does not roar in pentameters. And that's the problem: how do you get a rhythm which approximates the *natural* experience, the *environmental* experience?

We should pay attention to that word – 'roar' – its invocation of volume, and the clear suggestion that such volume is necessarily compromised or reduced if and when it tries to fit itself into another aesthetic culture.

But you see, even Walcott wrote poetry that roared with a beauty and a floridness that did not sit easily within English sensibilities. And it cost him – for even a poet as lauded and celebrated as he was, was occasionally sidelined by the English need to police volume.

In 2014 I became the first writer of colour to win the Forward Prize and much of the subsequent press made a fuss about this supposed accomplishment. I wasn't sure that I thought of it as an accomplishment. I thought about the black-American comedian Chris Rock, who has questioned the notion of 'black progress'. To believe in 'black progress' is to believe that black bodies were deserving of the discrimination and the segregation that they had faced before. To believe in the progress of the victimised is to believe that only now have they advanced to the point of deserving greater inclusion. For Chris Rock, to call even Obama's rise to the White House as evidence of black progress would be to accept the fallacy that no black man before, and certainly no fat black woman, had ever been worthy of the presidency. What we so often call 'black progress' according to Rock is simply white people acting less crazy. Or better still, it is white progress.

I felt very much the same in relation to the Forward Prize. I was not the first person of colour who deserved to win it. At the very least that distinction belonged to Walcott. In 2010, as his illustrious career was drawing to its close, it was widely assumed that the two friends and Nobel laureates, Derek Walcott and Seamus Heaney, would be going head to head for the prize. In the end – to much surprise – Walcott wasn't even shortlisted. Other people were not surprised at all. The chief judge of the Forward Prizes that year was Ruth Padel, Walcott's rival for the Oxford Professorship in Poetry. A year before, Padel had engaged in a messy and highly public smear campaign against Walcott. Still, it wasn't Padel who was the most outspoken of the judges. It was the poet Hugo Williams who provided the most telling statement:

> Walcott seems to have dropped off; this was not his best thing. I read his first book when I was 18. I thought it a bit florid, and I've stayed with that.

Walcott was outed for having Fat Black Woman ways. Walcott himself, while happy to embrace a Western aesthetic has commented on this kind of excess, this rapture, this volume, that so often creeps into Caribbean poetry. He writes:

> For tourists, the sunshine cannot be serious. Winter adds depth and darkness to life as well as to literature, and in the unending summer of the tropics not even poverty or poetry seems capable of being profound because the nature around it is so exultant, so resolutely ecstatic, like its music.

In 2010, his usually concealed Fat Black Womanness had worked against him. And if, as I suggest, such English condescension could be used against a poet with the clout of Walcott, how much more must it have been used, and used effectively, against poets whose names I would not even know to mention now – poets who have been successfully silenced, dismissed, unpraised. And this is what is at stake here.

It might interest you to know that Hugo Williams had similarly cutting remarks for the other Nobel laureate, Heaney, who did make it onto the short list. 'It's a brave effort,' said the judge. 'It's not his finest hour but nevertheless he's there.'

Hardly a ringing endorsement. Yet, it was not enough to keep Heaney off the shortlist, and it was not enough to prevent him from winning eventually. Walcott would go on that year to win the T. S. Eliot prize, and in four years I would go on to win the Forward Prize from a shortlist in which most bookies were predicting the winner would be none other than Hugo Williams himself. Is it petty and mean-spirited of me to admit this – that my victory over Hugo Williams that night, made me feel – to put it plainly – smug?

IV

If there is a poem that I do not read for fear of its volume, there is a poet in my lineage who I do not acknowledge enough for the same reason – the Jamaican poet and activist Staceyann Chin. It must have been at around the same time that I had met Walcott and he had told us about poetry not being a democracy. I had recently dropped out of university and with no degree and no career to claim I was embracing the vocation of writer.

Several stories had been written and I was only just beginning to feel my way into poetry. I knew the sequence of poems I wanted to write – portraits of Jamaican church women, and I had written perhaps the first three.

And then there came Calabash – the first staging of what would become one of the major international literary festivals. In that first year, its smallest staging, we were huddled under a tent at Jake's resort. There were whispers before Staceyann took to the stage. Someone near me, obviously a friend, said to another friend – 'She's back there – feeling nervous you know. The whole lesbian thing, and reading in Jamaica. She's just trying to gather her nerves.' And these two women held hands as if wishing and praying for strength for this poet.

I had never heard of or heard this lesbian Jamaican poet before. I gather most people in the audience hadn't either. This was the moment when she would scream her way into Jamaica's popular consciousness. There was a palpable and raw energy that textured the air the moment she walked up to the microphone. She was such a skinny thing – an Afro-Chinese-Jamaican woman rocking an Angela Davis afro. And there was something so nervous and vulnerable and exciting about her, the way she carried with her this energy that would never ebb. How could a woman so small, control the air so magnificently? She read her first poem and the energy grew into something magical and extraordinary. It is not hubris to say she was transforming Jamaica; my little island, which at the time was even more homophobic than it is now, was being held in the palm of her hand and being moved by a performance the likes of which the island had never experienced before. And she was so loud! Her poems were not so much recited as they were screamed – and yet, they always felt perfectly pitched. Nothing was excessive. This was poetry coming at its highest gale force, Brathwaite's prophesied hurricane of sound, and we were caught in its middle. Like a landscape that had just endured a hurricane, I knew that my poetry would forever carry the imprint of the storm. Useless branches were torn away. Something new was about to flourish. My poetry had been profoundly and forever changed.

Only now – a decade after that storm has passed, have I stopped to think about the nature of the change. Other poets had affected me before – Emily Dickinson, Lorna Goodison and W. S. Merwin – but I had encountered them on the page, relatively muted. The voice that I imagined as theirs was really my own. I encountered Staceyann on stage, in the dizzying decibels of her own volume. Her voice was her own – and this was what she gave to me – a voice, or at least the sense of it, and a range of performative gestures. I have never shouted at the decibels of a Staceyann Chin and yet she affected the volume at which I both read and wrote poems. What changed immediately was my performance; I would never read my own poems in the same way again, with an affected shyness that one was made to believe was the way serious poets read – eyes glued to the page on which we insist our poetry is rooted.

There was this small productive moment in my emergence as a poet that the old and oftentimes false barriers between performance poetry and written poetry did not exist for me. Inevitably, those barriers come back up; the institutions of poetry and our cultures of taste are invested in maintaining them – but there was that productive moment when I was open and receptive to a slam poet affecting my work just as much as the long dead Emily Dickinson. Performance teachers are often brought in to teach poets how to read their own poems – how to let the words rise off the page, but back then I was learning the lesson in reverse. I was beginning to wonder how we put sounds onto the page, how to write the volume I was so affected by.

In the direct aftermath of Staceyann's performance, her influence was embarrassingly obvious. My flailing hands for instance, and the ways I would walk to a lectern with a batch of papers, glancing only at the first line before tossing it to the wind and reciting the poem instead from memory. These had been her gestures and for a little while they had become mine. I'm not certain when I lost these, but I did. Yet I think there is still something of Staceyann in my voice.

In one of the poems that she loved to read a decade ago, performing it even on BET Def Poetry Jam – the young poet imagines herself in the future – the kind of woman she would like to become. 'If only out of vanity, I have wondered what kind of woman I will be.' She writes, 'I want to be forty years old, and weigh 300 pounds and ride a motorcycle in the wintertime, four hell-raising children and a 110-pound female lover who writes poetry about my life.'

What is so wonderful here is not only that she casts her present self as her future lover but that the self that she transforms into is none other than the Fat Black Woman, this embodiment of so many of Staceyann Chin's poetics – the impoliteness, the brazenness, the sheer volume of it.

I'm embarrassed now that I have hardly acknowledged the influence of Staceyann Chin who in polite and tasteful literary circles does not stand up well as a suitable influence. In the very next line of the poem 'If Only Out Of Vanity', Chin says, 'I want to be the girl your parents will use as a bad example of a lady'. I don't know much about that, but she certainly is, for many, the bad example of a poet. She has not gone on to publish a full collection. Her much awaited first book, when it finally did come out and to great success, was in fact a memoir. Though she was touring America, Africa and Asia, packing schools and auditoriums, appearing on slots on the Oprah Winfrey show, the poetry community had still dismissed her. No, they said. This is not poetry. It doesn't make sense to even try.

In 2014 I had the opportunity to read with Staceyann in Johannesburg. The night was billed as two Jamaican acts on one stage – but in truth, I was her opening act. It was one of those incredibly large stages you would imagine for a rock concert rather than a poetry reading. It opened onto a large football field. My reading did not go particularly well. It seems I had become the kind of poet whose volume does not demand immediate attention. I had become a poet without flailing hands because those hands needed to hold on to the books that I was reading from. I read my poems that night, but the audience never came forward to the stage. They remained in their little groups, congregated around the field. They continued their conversations until I was done. And then it was time for Staceyann Chin. All at once the little groups converged into a crowd. They moved as one to the stage. The old excitement that I myself had experienced years ago at Calabash was there again. She mostly read from the memoir she had written, but even her prose was pitched at the same volume with which she used to read poems. Again she was able to hold the crowd in the swell of her energy. In the end, she did read a few poems – haikus. Honestly, I thought they were terrible poems. I am certain that it isn't a fault of memory but the poems in Johannesburg were not the ones I had heard in Jamaica. These new poems were lazy, didactic – they lacked images. But to say these things, am I now judging her poetry through the same aesthetic lens that this essay has tried to challenge? Yes, perhaps I am. But I also know that she had given up. She had felt the brunt of rejection from the poetry gatekeepers for so long that these new poems no longer made even the smallest attempt to please them. By the time I met her again in South Africa, it was as if she had accepted that she would never publish a collection, that she was more of an activist than she was an author. It was activism then that required volume. Poetry didn't. So why write poems to win the approval of those so intent on ignoring her?

That night in Johannesburg, I felt a quality of loss which is a feeling that I need to think about. Remember – this was a night in which my own poetry had failed to spark anything in that crowd while Staceyann drew them all towards her and ignited a kind of fire. Why should I feel any loss, any sadness, any emotion that was textured with a sort of pity? Who was I to pity her?

I write this essay in praise of Staceyann Chin whose voice I insist, echoes inside my own – textures the edges of it.

I write this essay against a critical landscape, a reviewing discourse that still continues to heap accolades and praise onto poets for their restraint and their subtlety and their quietness, not stopping nearly enough to think how such praise can be racially loaded.

I write this essay in praise of the Fat Black Woman, her theories of brilliant bawling, and the beautiful rituals which she speaks up for – first night, third night, ninth night – all the sleepless droning red eyed wakes nights.

I write this essay in praise of volume.

Four Poems

PARWANA FAYYAZ

Forty Names

I

Zib was young.
Her youth was all she cared for.
These mountains were her cots
The wind her wings, and those pebbles were her friends.
Their clay hut, a hut for all the eight women,
And her father, a shepherd.

He knew every cave and all possible ponds.
He took her to herd with him,
As the youngest daughter
Zib marched with her father.
She learnt the ways to the caves and the ponds.

Young women gathered there for water, the young
Girls with the bright dresses, their green
Eyes were the muses.

Behind those mountains
She dug a deep hole,
Storing a pile of pebbles.

II

The daffodils
Never grew here before,
But what is this yellow sea up high on the hills?

A line of some blue wildflowers.
In a lane toward the pile of tumbleweeds
All the houses for the cicadas,
All your neighbors.
And the eagle roars in the distance,
Have you met them yet?

The sky above through the opaque skin of
Your dust carries whims from the mountains,
It brings me a story.
The story of forty young bodies.

III

A knock,
Father opened the door,
There stood the fathers,
The mothers' faces startled.
All the daughters standing behind them
In the pit of dark night,
Their yellow and turquoise colors
Lining the sky.

'Zibon, my daughter'
'Take them to the cave.'
She was handed a lantern.
She took the way,
Behind her a herd of colors flowing.
The night was slow,
The sound of their footsteps a solo music of a mystic.

Names:
Sediqa, Hakima, Roqia,
Firoza, Lilia, and Soghra
Shah Bakhat, Shah Dokht, Zamaroot,
Nazanin, Gul Badan, Fatima, and Fariba,
Sharifa, Marifa, Zinab, Fakhria, Shahparak, MahGol,
Latifa, Shukria, Khadija, Taj Begum, Kubra, Yaqoot,
Fatima, Zahra, Yaqoot, Khadjia, Taj, Gol, Mahrokh, Nigina,
Maryam, Zarin, Zara, Zari, Zamin,
Zarina,

At last Zibon.

IV

No news. Neither drums nor flutes of
Shepherds reached them, they
Remained in the cave. Were
people gone?

Once in every night, an exhausting
tear dropped – heard from someone's mouth,
A whim. A total silence again

Zib calmed them. Each daughter
Crawled under her veil,
Slowly the last throbs from the mill house

Also died.
No throbbing. No pond. No nights.
Silence became an exhausting noise.

V

Zib led the daughters to the mountains.

The view of the thrashing horses, the brown uniforms
All puzzled them. Imagined
The men snatching their skirts, they feared.

We will all meet in paradise,
With our honoured faces
Angels will greet us.

A wave of colours dived behind the mountains,
Freedom was sought in their veils, their colors
Flew with wind. Their bodies freed and slowly hit

The mountains. One by one, they rested. Women
Figures covered the other side of the mountains,
Hairs tugged. Heads stilled. Their arms curved
Beside their twisted legs.

These mountains became their cots
The wind their wings, and those pebbles their friends.
Their rocky cave, a cave for all the forty women,
And their fathers and mothers disappeared.

A Survival Prayer

I

Those summer nights in Kabul, tranquility
Was in the orchard of apricot trees:
In their images and shadows.
What happened to Uncle Najib?
What happened to the neighboring apple trees?

The nights are unknown,
The mornings are disturbed by the darkness,
Wake me up, father.
This is not the city
I live in. Neither is that one
My city, which I have called mine.

II

A long river flowing exhausted
Across the spring season,
A stream of coal-filled rocks.
It flows, flows,
Hitting the shores, where the tulips are born with thorns.
Though my mother says:

'The tulips' petals are the praying hands of a woman.'

The tulips are frozen deep down
Under the river,
I feel cold over my hands,
Cover me, mother.
This is not the nature
I was born with. Neither is it in my nature,
To survive this river.

III

I pray to the clouds
For rain.
Instead, the sound of shootings,
Some men scream,
Into the night.
The sound reaches my ears so fast,
I feel mortal again.
Hold my hands, brother. If there is a war again,
I will not pray for peace. Nor will I call it a war.

The Cursed Man

He owned two mansions, two barns,
The woman, who the *Khan* fell in love with at
First sight.

Her name was Sabar Gul, the *patience flower*.
She was living with her mother in a clay-made hut.

There was an oath passed between the elders,
Gul was engaged to her cousin since her childhood.
Therefore, the *Khan* could not ask for her.

In a series of dark nights and winter days,
Khan was driven to *Gul*,
Finally,

One midnight he pulled his horse and quietly
Seized *Sabar Gul* and took her to his private *Burj*, mansion.

Gul disappeared. A fable spread:
One of those middays as the summer sun was burning
Bright on the shuddering wheat fields,

And the
Farms were waiting for fall,
Sabar Gul, the daughter of that deceased *nek mard*, good man
Ran away with her *Mashuq*, beloved.

Gradually rumours spread in every village.

Though, the next day, *Khan* was back in the village with his horse,
Nothing was more pleasant than his secret feelings,
And all the rumours seemed pleasing. He thought.

Next dawn, before the women woke up to bake
Their breads and the shepherds to play their flutes,
Gul was brought back to her village.

She was left leaning, her back against the wooden door,
Unable to knock, she waited for the door to crack open.

The *Khan* looked around for a while,
Gazing at *Gul* – and her surroundings –
To protect her from any wild wolf.

The door opened, and the *Khan* raced behind the bushes
And mounted his horse.
He and his horse returned to their mansion.

She remained unseen around the village for
Months, her mother locked her in, far from
The villagers' sight, anger and horror.

Until people found out that
That night, in that dry night, under the moon,
The *Khan* was missing too, and so was his horse.

Sabar Gul's mother cursed him day and night,
Until the curse turned into a poison,
In the same season, a year later,

Khan's body collapsed on the ground,
After twelve days on his bed,
Khan died young and handsome.

My Grandmother's Ruby Ring

My grandmother wears a deep red ring,
A ruby set into a silver plate.

She lived in the valleys.
An orphan girl, herding her sheep in the fields.
A virgin: not yet menstruating, she became the bride
For another orphan. A ring was given to her
In a man's name, she was taken away.

She became a wife and lived in the city,
Caring for the man, his four brothers
His four sisters and their sad stories.

Seasons passed by, hardships:
She was separated from her husband
And went to live with her three boys and their families.

Throughout her separation,
She had always dreamed about her husband sitting
Under the shade of the apricot trees, or watering the
Tomato plants in the garden – she was *Zulaykha* and

He *Yosuf* – she always referred to him
As the prophet in her dreams.

She does not complain about the wounds over her hands.
A mother in law, a grandmother,
And gradually she became
A great-grandmother.
She had never shed a tear over the shattered clay roofs
Under the snowfalls.

Now her story is about an old woman waiting for death.
The ring goes to the one who washes her body.
only the woman who washes her well, dresses her properly and
Pays respect to her body would inherit her ring.

Aharon Appelfeld

(1932–2018)

GABRIEL JOSIPOVICI

THE ISRAELI NOVELIST Aharon Appelfeld died on 4 January. It would, however, be truer to say that he was one of the last of the great central European authors who lived and worked in the aftermath of the Austro-Hungarian Empire, and who include Musil, Hofmannsthal, Rilke, Wittgenstein, Kafka, Celan, Bernhard, Ingeborg Bachmann and Peter Handke. Writers whose first language was German but who, as Marjorie Perloff has rightly insisted, should be seen as a distinct group, very different from their north German counterparts – Mann, Brecht, Grass and the rest.

He was born in 1932 in Czernowitz, the chief city of Bukovina in what was then Romania and is now Ukraine, into an assimilated, wealthy, German-speaking Jewish family. 'The annual pilgrimage to the Mecca of culture, Vienna, was a feature of my early life,' he has said. Paul Celan, born in the same thriving metropolis eight years earlier, wrote in German all his life, though bitterly aware that his mother tongue had been contaminated by the Nazis and that to use it at all was to work with fatally tarnished tools. Appelfeld, whose mother was murdered when the Nazis moved into Bukovina in 1941 and who with his father was incarcerated in a camp, escaped, wandered in the forests of Eastern Europe for a year, was picked up by the Russian Army, eventually made his way, via Italy, to Israel. It was natural, then, that when he began to write, the language he would use would be Hebrew, but it was always a language he had to work at and for, and in a late interview he was still lamenting the fact that history had dispossessed him of his mother tongue. In his newly acquired language, however, he wrote – continuously and abundantly – mostly about the Europe of his childhood and youth, the coming of the Nazi nightmare, and how it affected the lives of those who survived.

His work is thus strikingly different from that of Amos Oz, A.B. Yehoshua and David Grossman, the best known of his contemporaries. Though Oz and Grossman have roots in Eastern Europe they were both born in Israel and their concerns are Israeli ones. Appelfeld, by contrast, is a European whose language happens to be Hebrew. That makes him, for me, a far more meaningful figure, someone with whom I can identify as I can identify with Kafka and Proust, whereas Oz, Yehoshua and Grossman feel as distant as Evelyn Waugh or William Faulkner, writers I admire but to whom I hardly feel close.

I first met him in 1982. Alerted by a brief *TLS* review of the first novel of his to appear in English, *Badenheim 1939*, I asked to review the next novel of his to appear in English, *The Age of Wonders*, and knew as soon as I opened it that I was reading something very special. The book is in two parts. In the first, written in the first person, we follow a boy growing up in an intellectual Jewish family in a small town in Germany or Austria in the thirties, trying to make sense of the arguments the adults are having about the increasingly fraught political situation. It ends with the cattle trucks rumbling away to the east. Part two, entitled 'Many Years Later, When Everything Was Over', is written in the third person and describes a visit to what must be the same town by a man called Bruno, now domiciled in Israel, who may or may not be the same as the boy of part one. It is one of the most powerful novels about the Holocaust that I know, not in spite of but because it passes over in silence what happens between 1942 and 1945. Dalya Bilu's masterly translation never allows us to imagine anything other than that this is a book written in English.

At the time John Levy ran an organisation called Friends of Israel Educational Trust, which brought English-language writers to Israel and Israeli writers to Britain to speak about their work in the informal setting of a private house. Oz came over, of course, and Carmi, the poet and editor/translator of the remarkable *Penguin Book of Hebrew Verse*. And so did Appelfeld. His talk was mesmerising. No one who has not had the privilege of hearing him can have any idea of the effect he had on his audiences. It was not just what he had to say. It was the man. The only way I can describe it is to say that there was a kind of transparency to him. Despite all he had been through he radiated a childlike innocence and an enormous gentleness. He had grown up speaking German with his parents, Yiddish with his grandparents, who were farmers in the Carpathians, Ruthenian with the serving girls, Polish and Russian in his forest wanderings, and Hebrew when he got to Israel. He had studied Yiddish and Yiddish culture at university, an act of piety, he later told me, towards a vanished culture. Somewhere along the way he had acquired English. He spoke slowly, with a strong accent, though whether Hebrew or German it was difficult to say, enunciating each word as if he had only just discovered it and was examining it with the wonder of a naturalist coming upon a hitherto unknown species. His eyes, behind his round glasses, twinkled as he spoke, and his bald head shone beneath the chandeliers.

He recounted his life, the happy childhood, the coming of the Germans, the death of his mother, his father and himself taken away and shut up in a camp, his escape and his life in the forest. 'When you are a child,' he said, beaming at us:

> you do not want to sit at a desk and work. You want to be out in the fields and the woods, playing and climbing trees. I was lucky. My childhood was spent in the forest, living with the gypsies and the horse thieves; they were wonderful story-tellers, it was wonderful for a child to listen to these stories. And then when I was big and wanted to study, who were my teachers? Martin Buber and Gershom Scholem. If I was minister of education everyone in Israel would have such a childhood, such an education.

At question time my mother asked: 'Did you ever find

out what happened to your father?' I was embarrassed for him and for her, but she clearly knew what she was doing. 'I will tell you,' he said, beaming at her:

> In Israel, in the first years, every day there were refugees arriving, and their names were always put in the paper. So every day I studied the paper to see if perhaps my father was one of them. And one day I saw his name. The paper said he was in a *kibbutz* in such and such a place, so I took a bus and went there. When I arrived and asked they looked at their list and they said: He is picking the fruit in that field over there. So I went to that field and it was full of fruit trees and in each tree a man. I walked down the rows and looked in each tree and then I came to one and there was my father.

Later, when I had come to know him, I asked: 'How did you get on with your father in later life?' 'It was difficult,' he replied. 'I was a grown man, I had been through so much, and he still treated me like a little boy.'

After he got to Israel he had a breakdown. But he slowly got himself together again, learned Hebrew and eventually got to university. He fought in all of Israel's wars, in 1948 and '56 and '68 and '73. Veterans, he explained to me, have by law to spend so many days a year back in the army, teaching and learning. It is good for the social life of the country. He was bitter about the way those who had been through the war in Europe were treated in the early days, and pleased that things had changed (due in large part, no doubt, to the writings of survivors like himself). But his view of Israel and its situation in the Middle East was coloured by his early experiences. 'They shut us up in ghettos and then they tried to exterminate us,' he said to me much later. 'And now they are trying to do it again.' 'Who is "they"?' I asked. 'Forty million Arabs,' he replied, and when I tried to argue that the Germans were a unified country and people, brainwashed by a fanatical leadership into carrying out a genocide that was purely gratuitous, whereas 'the Arabs' were a miscellaneous group of countries who would never agree on a common aim and that the Palestinians had a rightful grievance, he would not listen. Sadly, that led to a cooling of our friendship, a breach that was never healed.

But in the early eighties things were quite different. Israel was still genuinely struggling with how to reconcile peace with security, I was ignorant and innocent and Aharon was so obviously a lovely man – and a wonderful writer, whose work resonated with me in a way which that of few of my contemporaries did. 'Gabriel, I want to put you in my suitcase and take you back to Israel,' said that ardent Zionist in his extraordinary voice at the end of our first set of meetings in the wake of his evening talk. And though I demurred I did set about making plans to visit him. 'Do you like walking?' he had asked me, and as I packed my bags I wondered whether to take my walking boots. In the end I decided they would be too bulky, and it was just as well, for Aharon's idea of walking was to stroll very slowly for twenty-five metres, talking, then stop and talk face to face for ten minutes before strolling on for another twenty-five. In that way we would 'walk' out from his house in the new little town of Mevaseret Zion, built on the hills outside Jerusalem (the name means 'herald of joy to Zion'), into the desert and sit down under a tree, and he would talk. I thought of the opening of Plato's *Phaedrus*, where Phaedrus and Socrates sit in the shade of a tree in the heat of the day and listen to the cicadas as Socrates talks, and rejoiced in my good fortune.

He told me about his wars. He pointed to a hill and told me how many of his friends had died or been wounded trying to take it in 1948. He told me about his studies with Buber: 'He would slowly eat a bar of chocolate as he spoke to us about I and Thou. It was just after the war, we were all hungry all the time, and as he talked we could only think about the chocolate that was disappearing into his mouth.' He told me how he could never forget the look in his father's eyes when the Germans entered their house. 'It was not fear it was a feeling of betrayal,' he said, 'they had betrayed the German civilisation he worshipped.' He told me about his love for the work of Kafka and Kleist, 'and that tradition of pure, clean German prose, which does not look back, only forward, till the story is finished'. About the absurdity, as he saw it, of magical realism: 'When you cannot think of how to go on you say: "Out of his armpit a leg was growing. And from his big toe a beautiful woman came out."' He told me about his first short stories and his close association with a Labour publishing house. 'I was a man of the left for many years,' he said. 'But now that I am not, all these writers who have good consciences, like Oz – who was my pupil – or Yehoshua, point to me and say I am right wing and not fit to be talked to. So before I was ignored because I was a survivor and now I am ignored because I do not speak the liberal words they like to hear.'

Like all writers a part of him resented what he saw as the greater success of his contemporaries and refused to recognise how beloved and famous he himself was, winner of countless awards, both in Israel and abroad. Yet in another way he did, and was grateful for it:

> Here in Israel I can write and my work will appear in the paper and the next day I am stopped in the street: 'Mr Appelfeld, I want to thank you for saying what has been hidden inside me for so long.' 'Mr Appelfeld, I am sorry that your wife has died.' 'But my wife has not died.' 'You wrote that she had died.' 'No, I wrote a story. In the story the wife of the narrator has died. My wife is very well, thank you.' You cannot imagine, Gabriel, how it helps a writer to have his work published in the newspaper and everybody in the country reading it. That is how it is here in Israel.

His wife Judith comes from Argentina. She looked after Aharon and the three children with a warmth and love that were palpable. Alongside his writing, in the end only his family mattered and what a close-knit and loving family they were when I used to go and stay, when the children were growing up. Aharon, however, didn't work at home. Like a good central European he used a café in Jerusalem, only a few minutes away by bus, as his study. People even rang him up there, knowing they would nearly always find him. When I came to stay, though, he always made time for me, taking me round the Jerusalem he loved, the side streets, the bookshops, the religious quarter of Mea Shearim, which he responded to with a nostalgia for a long-vanished culture that only someone with his background could feel (it is a source of deep unease for secular Jews like Yehoshua, who in recent years has fled to Haifa, horrified by the increasingly shrill religious tone of the city his family had lived in for generations).

In the evenings we would stroll round the perimeter of Mevaseret Zion, which at the time housed a holding centre for immigrants recently arrived in Israel. 'Listen to the voices,' Aharon would say. 'See how many languages there are: Russian, Romanian, Polish, French, Ethiopian.' And, indeed, there were a large number of Ethiopians, recently arrived in Israel and bringing with them a culture totally different from both that of the Ashkenazi Jews of Eastern Europe who for long formed the ruling elite and of the Sephardi Jews of Iran, Iraq and north Africa, whose steady increase in numbers and sense of grievance at the way they were treated by the ruling elite would lead to the rise of Likud and (with some input from newly arrived Russian immigrants in the nineties) to the transformation of Israel into the increasingly chauvinist and aggressive entity we have come to know in recent years. Then, in the eighties, the Ethiopians were – to a romantic Zionist like Aharon at any rate – an exotic addition to the ethnic melting pot that was Israel; now they form a sad and increasingly disillusioned minority, treated as unwelcome outsiders only a rung above the non-Jewish illegal African immigrants who are treated as badly as possible by the authorities in the hope that they will decide to leave of their own accord.

One day Aharon said: 'Let's go and visit Dan Pagis.' The poet, also a native of Bukovina, was born two years before Aharon and, like him, was imprisoned by the Germans and escaped, like him he found his way to Israel, where he eventually became a professor of medieval Hebrew poetry at the Hebrew University. He is best known to the wider public for one short poem, 'Lines Written in Pencil in a Sealed Railway-Car':

> here in this carload
> I am eve
> with abel my son
> if you see my other son
> cain son of man
> tell him that

I had no idea he lived close by but in ten minutes we were there. Many of the houses in Mevasseret Zion have a garage as the ground floor. The Appelfeld's have turned theirs into a lumber room, but as we approached Dan Pagis's house Aharon looked through a little window, then stepped back and beckoned me to take a look for myself. Pagis had turned his garage into a study. He sat at a desk with his back to us, reading by the light of a table lamp. What made the scene so surreal was that the study also housed his car, which stood not a metre away from the desk in the cramped space.

The two greeted each other effusively in Hebrew but when Aharon introduced me switched at once to English. Pagis, it turned out, was reading his beloved George Herbert. 'There are many similarities between his poems and those of the medieval Hebrew writers,' he told me, with a smile as broad as Aharon's. I remember nothing more about the meeting, but the memory of that first peek into his garage will never leave me.

It's very difficult to work out the precise chronology of Appelfeld's books. He always maintained that he would write a new book, put it aside, write some others, then return to the first one, rewrite it and then publish it, and that as a result it meant little to ask when such and such a book was 'written'. No doubt there is some truth in that, but it also reflects his love of obfuscation, his penchant for stories that at best bore only a tangential relation to reality, but which over the years acquired a patina of truth just because they were so good. In any case, it seems to me that the books of his that were first published in English, in the eighties and nineties, by David Godine in Boston and Quartet Books in London – *Badenheim 1939*, *The Age of Wonders*, *The Healer*, *The Retreat* – are all of them masterpieces, among the finest works of fiction published in the second half of the twentieth century. The books that came after – an unending stream of novels and memoirs, culminating in *The Man Who Couldn't Stop Sleeping* (2017), books that have been highly acclaimed in America, France and Germany, are lesser things, dealing with the same themes but without the rich ambiguities of the earlier novels. That, of course, is a personal opinion. Good readers I know and respect admire them greatly, and they go on winning prizes, though I sometimes wonder if these are awarded for the worthiness of the content rather than the quality of the writing.

What I will always remember, though, is the excitement of reading those early books, the delight of meeting him and finding that for once a great artist and a wonderful human being could co-exist – and his generosity and kindness towards me. You always felt he was a man living in his own world, haunted by old ghosts, but that did not stop him responding with warmth and delight to those he trusted and was fond of, and I am sure he included me in that group. In the past few years I have often thought I should write before it was too late to tell him what he had meant to me and how absurd it was to lose a friend because of a political disagreement. Sadly, I never did, and now it is too late.

But not too late to reread the books. I open *The Age of Wonders* and at once it starts to work its magic on me. Listen:

> Many years ago Mother and I took the night train home from the quiet, little-known retreat where we had spent the summer. The coach was new, and on one of its rounded walls was a poster of a girl holding a bunch of cherries in her hand. Our places were reserved, the seats solid and comfortable with embroidered white antimacassars on their headrests. The compartment door was open and a girl, very like the one in the poster, stood there with a wooden tray in her hands. She stood in the doorway for a long time and then suddenly, as if set in motion by some external command, started walking down the aisle serving coffee and cheesecake.

A Sequence & Six Poems

CRAIG RAINE

You Plural, You Singular

All the way up Everest,
there is litter –
litter and dead bodies.

But at the summit,
a flag's essential tremor.

During the descent,
you need to see your feet.

Do not cry
when someone falls to their death.
Tears make it difficult
to see your Scarpa Phantoms.

Someone.
Two people –
Lamps and Jezza –
Lamps then Jezza.
The same sudden crevasse.

But you try to hold back the tears.

*

Base camp:
how strange to miss
the sensation of lipstick,
lips taut over your teeth,
a moist mouth
clumsily kissing itself.
To miss the close-up
of a happy mouth –
seen in a Gucci compact –
restricted view,
out of context.
Before all this happened.

What does it mean?
Grief in disguise. He says.
He can be very intelligent.
You have always known that.

Base camp
with its lines of washing like bunting.
Its heaps of equipment –
harnesses, hexs, crampons,
prussiks, cylinders –
piled up like plunder.
Waiting to be sorted, sifted,
tested, set aside, discarded.

You preferred Lamps.
But you liked them both.

They were part of the group DNA.
Lamps shaking out
his thick heavy hair
otherwise tight to his head in a hair-band.
As if in denial.

You have to learn to let go. He says.

Simon Yates cutting
the rope on Joe Simpson.
Aron Ralston amputating his own arm.

Yes to both. He says.

*

He says. Your fiancé David.
He believes in renunciation.
In walking away.
Top climber.
Before that, philosophy at Cambridge,
at Trinity, failed to get a first
and took up yoga.
Then rock climbing,
then mountains.

Kilimanjaro. Mont Blanc. K2.
Everest. Degrees of difficulty.

Mountains: all about getting a first.
He wants to be top.

A puzzle.
A worry.
Why are you part of his team?
Of course you can climb.
But the way women piss.
Zips the length of your bottoms:
no need to take off your boots.
But that's the same for men.
The pee funnel takes practice:
not just the emplacement,
you have to control velocity.
Like breath control for a singer.
A steady pressure for longer,
then nothing. Dead stop.
And you have to pee.
You can't not pee
because you have to drink.
Dehydration will kill you.

So David,
undemonstrative David,
must love you. Otherwise

you wouldn't be here.

Even though he would leave you behind.
                    *

A handsome couple,
a beautiful couple.
An American
in her mid-thirties,
married to a Russian.
Her second marriage.
They believe in pure climbing.
'It is a philosophy.'
No oxygen. No sherpas.
'It is religious climbing.'

She didn't look at us.
She looked at the screwgate
in her strong fingers,
as if it were a god.
A little god,
a specialist god.
The Himalayan god
Gore-Tex. Or Cocona
who rules over pitons and harnesses.
And all the time she talked,
she never smiled. Not once.
'The way up is also the way down.'
The Russian second husband
said nothing,
smiled seriously.

The latest equipment.
Like models in a catalogue.
People without a past.
David called them
Dolce and Gabbana.
They never said their names.

They had already climbed Lhotse
by the difficult route.
                    *

The team found her
on the Khumba Ice Fall
at 18,000 feet.

Our second attempt on the summit.
A week after Lamps and Jezza,
before the weather closed.

No trace of the Russian husband.

Even from a distance,
something was wrong.
Her body belly-up,
in a circumflex
like an upturned suitcase.
She looked broken.

Hypothermia: fatally cold,
you feel a fever of heat.
She had removed
her jacket, her mittens and inners.
Her mask had gone.
Her face lay on her loose dark hair,
a three-quarter moon,
bent like a mask.

She was still alive.

'*I am an American.
You must help me.*'

Her eyes were all pupil.
She could see nothing.
They were like pieces of coal.
Losing their shape.

Her face and hands
were drained, colourless,
semi-transparent polyurethane
where the moisture had frozen.
Her features wiped clean.

Neither eyelashes nor eyebrows.
Her invisible lips moved invisibly.

'*Help me. I am an American.*'

The three sherpas moved away,
waiting to move past her
and on to the summit.
They kept their distance.
Repudiation. Pragmatism.
David asked their opinion.
They looked at each other.
'She dead. Go on now.
Or freezing.'
It wasn't obvious which one had spoken.

David: 'There's nothing we can do.'

'We can't leave her,' you said.
'She's alive.'

'But she's going to die.'

'*Help me. I am an American.*'

A truth held to be self-evident.

After five minutes,
the group moved on.

Maybe less than five minutes.

A lot less than five minutes.

It was the cold that decided.
                    *

You couldn't pass her body.
When it came to it.
When you came to it.

So they went on without you,
up to the summit,
and you came down alone
with one of the sherpas.
All the sherpas had made the summit before.

You hadn't helped her.
There was nothing you could do.
This time you could see your feet.

Something was rubbing in your left boot.
At base camp,
you twisted off your 8000s.
A blister on the side of your big toe,
caused by the seam of your liner sock.
It was a gemstone. Rose quartz.

You could see it as beautiful,
as semi-precious jewellery.

Or you could feel it as pain.
It was up to you.

You knew David would leave you.
That you had left him.

Because of another woman.

*

There was something else.
Something impossible at that height.
Something you keep to yourself.

Something you keep from yourself.

A butterfly.

Just above Base Camp,
a butterfly's cerebral palsy,
flickering, blundering
beautifully past.
Out of the blue,
into the blue.

Like a little fire. Like a flag.

*

There were two kinds of you.
There was you plural
and you singular.
You plural was like 'one'.
As in 'one doesn't see butterflies at 16,000 feet'.

Small Change

The opaque bird bath.
Black ice on the brick path

like the cellophane ink spill
from a kid's conjuring set.

Dead still. Everything stet.
Extinction everywhere, until,

escaped from the farthing
into my garden,

this tiny teapot of a wren,
tipping, then tilting again,

the perfect host,
topping up

all the invisible ghosts,
holding out invisible cups.

A dolls' house heaven,
where all is forgiven.

Mirror

The intelligence of mirrors.
Brilliant. Infallible. Unhesitating.
They understand immediately.
Yes, they say to everything. I see.

The caterpillar's bellydance.
A seething double helix of starlings
like a matador's cape.

Snowflakes under the street-lamp:
tinsel, silverfish, a shoal
shifting, steady in the current.

A herd of pianos for sale:
Bechsteins, Steinways, Yamahas.
Silent, suddenly plangent, shaking,
lonely, longing for footsie.
Wanting a touch.

How clear the mirrors are.
How well they explain.
Their cold sunlit November day:
iron trees, iron birds, iron brambles.
The stillness of their photograph.

The meteorology of mirrors.
Clouds. Sleepy with algae. Mottled.
Maculate. Blots. Blotches. Condensations.
Through the glass, darkness.

Arte Povera

Cleansed of sand in the sink,
sepia squid in its black ink.
Conté crayon,
rough charcoal, wet slate:
tachiste perfection
of the empty plate.

On the toilet bowl,
another Dubuffet masterpiece,
two coarse marks, improvised,
frayed, painterly, bold.

Dirty studio walls,
a colour chart, the Pantone
daubs of Francis Bacon,
careless and careful.

Green pea puree: the chef,
an artist with a palette knife,
applies an expert smear,
like a straight razor.

Over a bald spot, thick
stiff brush strokes.
Varnish. Papyrus.

Body hair:
black on white,
a starved brush,
not everywhere,
just here. And here. And there.
Indisputable. Exactly right.

This grey wash. This long stain.
The iron curtain of the rain.

Miracles

The bull's waxed
Salvador Dali moustache,

the giraffe's potato print,
its crazy pavement,

long in the tooth,
the walrus in her wet suit,

a comic creature
like a joke-shop Nietzsche.

And this tortoise advertised
by its sandwich board:

fastidious features tell
of Bertrand Russell,

the awkward
arthritic claws

accented, one half
acute, the other grave,

two fir cones,
slow, rheumatic stones.

The tortoise
its own suitcase,

poorly packed.
Or perfectly packed:

perfect for hibernating,
for patiently waiting...

until I saw
my late mother-in-law,

as if she didn't die
after all, head held high,

out of the water,
seized by laughter,

her rubber bathing cap
and tightened chinstrap,

her minimal breast-stroke,
so the Cherwell broke

in modest ripples,
reflecting her wrinkles

(anointed with Nivea cream).
A rite of spring. A sacred theme.

Caffeine

In my dream,
I had to write about caffeine.

The last question of three.
I had written two answers already,

but this was the third,
deliberately hard.

The question knew for a certainty
I had no chemistry.

But I know
how to make a ristretto.

So, a makeshift
answer in the five minutes left.

Oiled beans sound
like maracas: ground

to gravel, fluffed
and softened to snuff.

A Doppler shift, an effect
the ear learns to detect.

Down
packed down.

Drops of aubergine
coaxed from a machine.

Or two nails, long, black,
twisted, like religious relics.

The espresso sheen
of *encre de Chine*.

This dark molten metal,
a cinnamon nap when it settles.

Our taste for the tart,
for the beaten heart,

for the bitter,
like a taste for failure.

Improbable,
acquired. Inevitable.

In the end,
the end.

Sipped without sugar.
With pleasure.

(The allotted time vanished
before I could finish.)

Falò Delle Vanità

Firenze 1497

The Duomo warps behind the torch.
Crowds gather to watch
destruction and feel its scorch.

Hell at second hand,
fanned by the November wind.
Torn fire tufts. Pulsing brands.

Squirming flames.
Hothouse chrysanthemums,
orpiment, Dominican browns.

Verrocchio's bronze bell,
La Piagnona, tolls.
Sound carries and calls

the faithful far and near,
brings to every ear
the sacrament of fear.

Savonarola's eyes are hard
with renunciation. Nothing spared:
not a trinket, not a playing card,

not a Botticelli drawing,
not a silken drawstring,
not a single silver florin.

(A year later, for its sins,
La Piagnona as recompense
was flogged the length of Florence.)

And nothing has changed.
The ways of fire are strange.
It burns on, unseen, deranged,

consuming women who weep
for their dead in their sleep,
unblinking goldfish, botox sheep,

the body builder's challah,
that tattooed torso, red-and-yellow,
like a court card in Valhalla.

Even your heartbreak of hair,
a ghost of grey smoke (See! There!)
caught in this comb, then held in the fire.

'the things of earth are not objects'

Two Takes on the Poetry of A. R. Ammons

The Complete Poems of A.R. Ammons, Vols 1 & 2, ed. Robert M. West (Norton) $100

1. Vidyan Ravinthiran

A. R. (ARCHIE RANDOLPH) AMMONS grew up dirt-poor, subsistence farming in North Carolina. At twenty-nine, he published his debut, *Ommateum*, with a vanity press. It didn't sell: he claimed the royalty for the first year was four four-cent stamps. Later, of course, he won it all, got a teaching job, and was acclaimed by heavyweight critics, including Harold Bloom (for whom he wrote a poem) and Helen Vendler. Her introduction is reprinted in both volumes of this overwhelmingly gargantuan *Complete Poems*. It's as if the poet has been knighted, with a touch of the sword on both shoulders. We lovers of Ammons have had to cobble together, till now, our own boxsets out of reprints and secondhands (my copy of *Garbage*, fittingly, arrived from Amazon collied and smutched). Here, at long last, all in one package, are the long masterpieces – besides *Garbage*, there's *Sphere*, and my favourite, *Tape for the Turn of the Year* – the genuinely amusing *Really Short Poems* ('Their Sex Life': 'One failure on / Top of another'; 'Coward': 'Bravery runs in my family') – and, glittering like pebbles on the beach, shorter poems totally new to me.

Where to start? With, in my opinion, his most beautiful single lyric, 'Hymn', which appeared in Ammons's second book, *Expressions of Sea Level* (1964). He was brought up in the Pentecostal Fire-Baptised Holiness Church (!) and the index to Volume 1 lists, besides this poem, 'Hymn II', 'Hymn III', 'Hymn IV' and 'Hymn V'. Like Walt Whitman, he professes his wide love for all living and even unliving things: 'though I have looked everywhere / I can find nothing lowly / in the universe: // [...] moss, beggar, weed, tick, pine, self, magnificent / with being!'. 'Hymn' is also shaped by the poet's Romantic yearning for both 'unity & diversity: how / to have both: must: / it's Coleridge's / definition of a poem':

> I know if I find you I will have to leave the earth
> and go on out
>   over the sea marshes and the brant in bays
> and over the hills of tall hickory
> and over the crater lakes and canyons
> and on up through the spheres of diminishing air
> [...]
> And I know if I find you I will have to stay with the earth
> inspecting with thin tools and ground eyes
> trusting the microvilli sporangia and simplest coelenterates
> and praying for a nerve cell
> with all the soul of my chemical reactions

'And if I find you I must go out deep into your far resolutions / and if I find you I must stay here with the separate leaves'. Though Ammons writes poems to a 'you' closer to the reader, this one's pitched at a god, or the shadow of one, understood as both transcendent and immanent; the spiritual, or what remains of it, is defined in opposition to the world of the senses, but also (necessarily) evoked in material terms.

Helen Small writes that 'an allusion to science in contemporary literature is not simply an allusion to science; it is also an allusion to the authority of science with respect to certain kinds of narrowly defined truth'; Robert Crawford finds in modern poetry 'a wish or instinct to extend the range of verse while at the same time acknowledging a certain risked awkwardness in using scientific vocabulary'. Ammons majored in science at Wake Forest University; yet his wilfully off-balance Latinisms are also, surely, a nod to Milton. The speaker's transit 'up through the spheres of diminishing air' recalls the wandering of Satan in *Paradise Lost*, and it's to be noted that an adjective from Milton's 'On Shakespeare' captures at one point in *Garbage* a vision of 'everything / assimilated to star-ypointing song'. There remains a critical issue with US poets announcing their intention to 'make it new', and critics (often American ones, it can get tribal) taking them too wholly at their word. 'I've done what I could,' Ammons wrote in 1992, 'to wipe out most / some of the western traditions by failing to refer to them... I hate all alluding that alludes.' But should we believe him? Ammons is full of it – allusion, that is. He mocks, admiringly, Stevens, to whom he was often compared, and 'blithering Yeats'; mentions L-A-N-G-U-A-G-E poetry; tells A. E. Housman, or 'Housey', that he wishes he'd got what he wanted out of life; parodies Eliot – 'sit down by this big rock / and if in a year you're / still not bored, I'll show you // something really interesting' – and I'm pretty sure that one of the special effects of 'Surfacing Surface Effects' owes something to Hopkins: 'A small moon nearly melted in the almost-morning / night, I arise and thank God I can get up'.

Ammons writes very short lines, and very long ones, and uses his trademark colon to establish, at its best, a new, unique 'prosetry' (his word): a parataxis which may pass, if you squint, for logical argument. 'This stanza compels / its way along: a / break will humble it': the cola, line breaks and stanza breaks, preserve in print the poet's defeats of confidence, which are also junctures at which a new thought may arise. (Elizabeth Bishop worried about the 'blank verse moo' of Wallace Stevens, and I was struck by Ammons also finding in that poet a mode of locomotion to disdain: 'Mr Stevens's lines! // laid like a railbed, tie after tie, / with no sign of integrated / progression but two stiff pieces of / stretched iron'.) Ammons can also be stridently, or offhandedly, slangy, irreverent, vulgar – 'Confessional Poem': 'Let me be honest with you: / in spite of everything I have / a (oh my) penis'. Yet he wishes, above all, to connect the everyday violences of our self-assertion with the epochal 'saliences' and 'crests' of the biosphere – he cares about the past, seeing it deeply alive in the mutations of the present: 'There is / memory enough in the rock, unscriptured history in / the wind, sufficient identity in the curve / of the valley'; 'we are dealing with a splintery weave of / surface which contains instances of the / present but also what is ancient and come / again.'

This explains his allusiveness, his performance of variations on the old orders. One section of 'February Beach', for example, rewards scansion – old-style literary appreciation. 'Warm days since / have intervened, / softened // the surface':

evaporated
the thaw
   and let grains loose: now

x /   /   / x / x /
the white grains drift against the dunes
x   / x x / x / x
and ripple as if in summer,
/ x   x /   / / x
hiding the deep hard marriage
x /   x /
of sand and ice:

A Williamsesque line is allowed to, gently, rhyme: 'thaw' and 'now' move the verse towards a memory of previous forms. Three-stress sequences combine with iambs: a weave of sound aligns 'grains' and 'dunes' (internal rhyme); 'drift', 'dunes' and 'deep' (alliteration); the collocations, with others, of 'drift', 'ripple' and 'as if', and 'hiding' and 'ice' (assonance). Though Ammons can be cussedly unshapely, even commenting on it – breaking off, say, to remark several lines ending on 'the' – this is one manoeuvre within a larger investigation of poetic and perceptual structures.

On the one hand, it's the American experiment in democracy, dramatised by so many writers, in vernacular diction and new-fangled open forms; but – I keep coming back to the Romantics – Ammons also inquires into the beautiful and the sublime: 'the shapes nearest shapelessness awe us most, suggest / the god'. When he wants, he can shape, hew, chisel, with the best of them:

I sat by a stream in a
perfect – except for willows –
emptiness
and the mountain that
was around,

scraggly with brush &
rock
said
I see you're scribbling again
   ('Classic')

This would emanate an absolute Zen clarity – were it not for that 'scraggly' phrase 'was around', and a carefully weighed, though spontaneous-seeming, interjection: 'except for willows'. Ammons inherits the stances of an inspiration-centred verse, but makes them down-to-earth, loveable, turning his speaker into a naïf who pursues impossible conversations with the elements, trees, animals, brooks and astral beings. 'The mountains said they were / tired of lying down / and wanted to know what / I could do about / getting them off the ground'; 'Some nights I go out to piss / among the big black scary shrubs: / the tinkling stars / don't seem to mind.' Here, as with that 'deep hard marriage' of ice and sand, what is sought is a language of relationship which could replace a lexis of conquest, and self-interested exploitation, of the world's resources.

Ammons may lament 'a waste of words, a flattened-down, smoothed- / over mesa of styrofoam verbiage; since words were / introduced here things have gone poorly for the / planet': but he isn't finally, the sort of eco-poet who treats humans as evil doers wild to ruin a primal harmony. We are of nature, part of it, and this is felt throughout the conversation poems I've mentioned. 'Ballad', for instance, where Ammons asks a willow 'what it wanted to know: the willow said it / wanted to know how to get rid of the wateroak / that was throwing it into shade every afternoon at 4 o'clock'. (Which also seems to me a fine, cunning poem on the politics of identity: 'I can't take you for a friend because while you must / be interested in willowness, which you could find nowhere / better than right here, / I'll bet you're just as interested in wateroakness'). Two of the really short poems provide glimpses of an ideal reciprocity, an unfallen state where competition cannot enter and existence is no longer transactional: 'Birds are flowers flying / and flowers perched birds'; 'The reeds give / way to the // wind and give / the wind away'. The same phrase haunts 'Late Romantic' – 'how can we give ourselves away if we're not separate / enough to be received' – combining the ways we talk about ourselves with discussion of global warming: 'change the glacier's loneliness and the ice melts'.

Ammons's craving for unity in multiplicity is precedented, but he makes a distinctively stateside leap from creative 'forms' to the 'forms' of society, or government; asking, in a passage from *Sphere*, what his readers 'expect from a man born and raised in a country whose motto is *E / pluribus unum?*' In 'Pray Without Ceasing', first published in 1973, he writes explicitly of the war in Vietnam: 'the Buddhist nun burns for the peace / her ashes will achieve: // the village woman coming home finds / her shack afire, her / son & husband shot'. Yet moments like these are exceptions, in a poet wary of partisan commitments: 'I've proved Emerson unimaginably // wrong: one *can* live in one's time, / and lucky for it, with no involvement // in its politics: / I love the chicanery, / fraudulence, expedience, greed of // the political (read, human) world'. Rather, in Ammons, politics, philosophy, and ecological awareness come together in a shared, multiform, register-hopping language, which can be highbrow one moment, then nose-thumbing – systematic and detail-rich.

My quotation concerning Coleridge, and diversity, is part of a broader political swerve in *Tape for the Turn of the Year*, and West's useful note tells us Ammons originally tied the idea to Lyndon Johnson's 'State of the Union' address. Though shorn of this reference, the final poem preserves the association:

what a celebration! our
little earth
united, shining in peace,
   hate managed,

>   rerouted:
>   the direction thru
>   history is clear:
>   unity amassing larger
>   & larger territories,
>   till now
>   neighborhoods of nations
>   meet
>   under the name 'United
>   Nations'

Ammons steps hearteningly beyond literary chatter – pressing, always, for a larger view. Reading him can be rather like moving to the side of things at a conference, or literary festival ('both in and out of the game', writes Whitman, 'and watching and wondering at it'), to take a cold-eyed anthropological survey of the room. The tribes agitating for power, the condensation of workable intimacies out of pre-fabricated gossip: 'hate managed, rerouted', 'unity amassing larger / & larger territories'. But Ammons doesn't take for granted, or even really desire, a superior, maybe snobbish, viewpoint. His increasingly diaristic verse (Ammons improvised *Tape*, from day to day, on a narrow strip of adding machine paper) doesn't omit his own spikes of resentment, grumpy lust, even those periods of insecurity as to the worth of all his endeavours – 'last night, after / anger & a family tiff, I / suffered a loss & breakage / of spirit, blankness / as of plateaus'. A series of poems from the 1972 *Collected* begin with the same phrase: 'I can tell you what I need is a good periodontist'; 'I can tell you what I need, what I need / is a soft counselor'; 'I can tell you what I need is / money'.

Returning to *Tape*, one can't take at face value that po-faced paean to globalisation, appearing as it does not far from this delicious description of symbiotic nature – the poet out in the sticks, disparaging of urban elites:

>   when I stooped to pick
>   up the turtle,
>   I seen a sight: his back
>   was hazy with
>   mosquitoes, thick
>   as they could
>   stick,
>   bumming a, now mind you,
>   ride on a turtle's back!
>   saving their wings
>   & certain
>   sometime they'd be
>   brought to water:
>   didn't see anything
>   like that in NY:
>   economy, full use
>   of possibility

'Most of our writers live in New York City,' writes Ammons – this is from, to give the full title, 'Sphere: the Form of a Motion' – 'there in the abstractions of squares and glassy / floors they cut up and parcel out the nothingness they / think America is.' Which brings to mind the recent election, and its result. Ammons speaks for the heartland, but he also discusses – in a uniquely unmoralising way – the circulations of global capital, and money's power over individual lives. I mentioned his scratty upbringings; later, he became vice president of his father-in-law's glassware company, and while we might link him to Stevens as a philosophical poet, they also both combined the writing life with the business life. Stevens worked for an insurance company; his poetry is metaphysical, but with the executive's hard-nosed questing, always, for the baseline statement (he was also politically conservative). The businessman wants to – ghastly word – grow his business, at the expense, necessarily, of others; the pure capitalist believes that herein lies the only possible transition from self-interest to creativity. When Ammons gets to talking about history, or evolution, or nation states, economics is never far away – though he's no advocate for Spencer's 'survival of the fittest'.

'Nucleus' asks – it's the first line – 'how you buy a factory', then describes how, in the Ammons's language of glimmeringly diagrammed processes, to:

>   determine the lines of
>   force
>   leading in and out, origins, destinations of lines;
>   determine how
>   from the nexus of crossed and bundled lines
>   the profit is
>   obtained, the
>   forces realised, the cheap made dear,
>   and whether the incoming or outgoing forces are stronger

Is it Ammons's background in the natural sciences that has him use the word 'force' so neutrally – without a whiff of Foucault? (He certainly recognises power when he sees it, commenting for example that even 'philosophy gives clubs to / everyone, and I prefer disarmament'.) *Tape for the Turn of the Year* expands Maslow's hierarchy of needs, from 'get food: / get water: / get sex:' to 'bank account, nice car, / good address, retirement / plan, investment portfolio' – and I don't think an easy irony is all that's intended. Ammons grants (this in 'One: Many'):

>   how enriching, though unassimilable as a whole
>   into art, are the differences: the small-business
>   man in
>   Kansas City declares an extra dividend
>   and his daughter
>   who teaches school in Duquesne
>   buys a Volkswagen, a second car for the family

I'm reminded of a passage in Tom Paulin's study of Thomas Hardy – which I read as an undergraduate, delighted a critic was allowed to say such things – where, analysing 'During Wind and Rain', he remarks wonderfully of the family's losses, their 'clocks and carpets and chairs / On the lawn all day, / And brightest things that are theirs', that these lines get into the poem that pride in ownership which everybody feels. Ammons's wife Phyllis is a quiet, repeated, welcome presence in the poems, 'as / solid as a jug or judge', and she, too – to reverse a sexist aphorism of Kafka's – tethers him to the finite: 'my wife says there / are so many niches / today where you / can make money'. Elsewhere, he grouses: 'Why is it that doctors expect to be paid for their / time and lawyers and bowling coaches for their / time but nobody expects to pay a poet', concluding, 'I guess poets // are supposed to be so used to poverty they don't need / any money'. Born poor, Ammons always remained aware of what's called, depressingly, and often to shut interesting people up, the real world.

Which doesn't mean accepting common sense as the way to go – becoming hard-headed. In Ammons's most famous poem, 'Corsons Inlet', he walks by the sea: inspired, or just out for a breath of fresh air? Either way:

> the walk liberating, I was released from forms,
> from the perpendiculars,
>   straight lines, blocks, boxes, binds
> of thought

Which resembles an ideal freedom, comparable with Joyce's flight from the nets of 'nationality, language, religion'. Ammons touches – it's 1962 – on war paranoia: 'no arranged terror: no forcing of image, plan, / or thought: / no propaganda, no humbling of reality to precept'. Keats said the poet should become a chameleon, even a nobody, a thoroughfare for all possible thoughts – Ammons tries to actually write by this method.

'Saliences' (a key word, in his work) states the time-paradox we live by, and which he returns to over and over: 'The reassurance is / that through change / continuities sinuously work / cause and effect / without alarm'. ('Local Antiquities': 'only / changing with change // stays beyond things / and us, mocks change's / mocking changes'.) This would be soupy stuff, were it not for the poet's up-close inscapes: 'the kept and erased sandcrab trails'; 'minnows left high on the tide-deserted pocket, / fiddler crabs / bringing up gray pellets of drying sand, / disappearing from the air's faster events'. It's the last line there that does it – bouncing from journal-jottings back into the shine of abstraction. (Like Stevens, Ammons knows that philosophical language has its own sensuous appeal.) Ammons excels at these snapshot-utterances – peculiarly particular, particularly peculiar, or just outright visionary: 'a marvelous morning / dull gray aflood with the possibility of light'; 'the caterpillar sulls on the hot macadam // but then, risking, ripples to the bush'; 'it's April 1 / the willow's yellow's / misting green'; 'balloons in inexperienced hands worry / me; I stagger into rushes of loss when they nod upward'.

Ammons is a realist: 'I knew an old woman who knew when that time / had come and that's what she told me, it's hard to hope / when there is no hope: she, naturally, died'. (Those commas, around 'naturally'!) But his verse can also be so clearly and unironically heartening, that I wish it were read by those who consume self-help manuals in droves. He speaks, sometimes, often, reassuringly, placing a hand on the reader's shoulder – again, resembling Whitman, when that poet breaks with the braggadocio, and says, quietly, in an alcove, as it were, of the Brobdingnagian yawp: 'It is not upon you alone the dark patches fall, / The dark threw its patches down upon me also'. 'A light catches somewhere,' Ammons tells us:

> to find a place to break out elsewhere:
> this light, tendance, neglect
> is human concern working with
> what is: one thing is hardly better
> or worse than another: the
> split hair of possible betterment makes
> dedication reasonable and heroic:
>
> the frail butterfly, a slightly
> guided piece of trash, the wind takes
> ten thousand miles

I'm aware that to isolate these moments from the vast, noisy weather systems of the poet's thinking, with their circulating movements of uncertainty, fear and irresolution, may be to sentimentalise. Yet Ammons can be as blatant as to announce, in 'Loving People', that 'people are / losing propositions', until 'you decide / to decide to love'; an actual sonnet appears on page three hundred and thirty of the second volume: 'Love surgent, equipped with the direction / of sail, is matchless'. Once the reader had to hunt in out-of-the-way bookshops, or succumb to Amazon's corporate dominion: the risk, now, is of such frankly touching verse disappearing into the, yes, deeply, densely enthralling morass of the overall project. Vendler suggests a new *Selected*, hewn from the newly collated oeuvre – a fine idea.

2. Ian Pople

'It was when my little brother, who was two and a half years younger than I, died at eighteen months. My mother some days later found his footprint in the yard and tried to build something over it to keep the wind from blowing it away. That's the most powerful image I've ever known.'
— A.R.Ammons

A. R. AMMONS was born into a poor, white, subsistence farming family near Whiteville, North Carolina in 1926. The house he was born into had no electricity and no indoor toilet. During that childhood, three other siblings were born and died young. His father's venture into commercial tobacco farming failed with Ammons was seventeen. Perhaps unsurprisingly, Ammon's Pentecostal Christianity didn't last out his teens. And was, according to Helen Vendler in her introduction to these volumes, substituted with 'the universal and inflexible laws of the universe in disciplines from the bacteriological to the astronomical', i.e. science. After wartime service in the navy, where he learned to type, the GI Bill enabled Ammons to go to Wake Forest University, where he graduated with a BSc in General Science. After graduation and marriage, Ammons was firstly an elementary school teacher and principal; then, initially reluctantly but ultimately quite successfully, he became a sales manager in the company run by his father-in-law, where he rose to become Executive Vice President. After this, he spent the rest of his working life teaching in universities, particularly Cornell.

Ammons first wrote poetry during night shifts in the navy; poetry which Vendler describes as 'inept' and 'varying from the sentimental to the comic'. At this time, too, Ammons come to 'an interior illumination' concerning the forces of nature as opposed to the forces of a God, 'I began to apprehend things in the dynamics of themselves – motions and bodies… I was de-denominated'. As a result of this illumination, Ammons later commented that what he tried to do in his poetry was 'a further secularisation of the imagination'. However, he still believed that 'the spiritual has been with us and will remain with us as long as we have mind'.

Vendler comments that, 'Ammons' first two books were uncertain ones'. Coming to these poems now, what emerges from them is a sense of the gestural, as though they reach out to something slightly beyond them; as in this, the opening of 'I Came in a Dark Woods Upon', 'I came in a dark woods upon / an ineffaceable difference / and oops embracing it / felt it up and down mindfully / in the dark / prying open the knees to my ideas'. As Vendler notes, Ammons embraced the colloquial early, and that sense of the empirical Ammons addressing the reader is present in much of Ammons's poetry. Here, even as Ammons nods to both Dante and Robert Frost, the poem also communicates the sheer enjoyment of being in the natural world which characterises much of Ammons's poetry. Perhaps it is expecting too much of the young poet that he elucidate 'ineffaceable difference' further and weave it in a more integrated way into the trajectory of poem – a poem which later goes on to state, 'The dryads took body in the oakhearts / The Angels shuttered their wintry peepholes'. And a number of the early poems have this tendency to pick an apercu and then both push it at the reader and also avoid its consequences. Poems in these early books also have rather gestural titles, such as 'Heterodoxy with Ennui' or 'Paradox with Variety', or even, and this from his first book, 'I Assume the World Is Curious About Me'. This latter poem is certainly filled with deflating irony, but even so.

It is with his third book, *Corsons Inlet*, and its wonderful title poem, that Ammons seems to settle into 'the American grain'. In the title poem, Ammons walks along a tidal inlet, observing and commenting on the world of the shoreline, and his own place there. As he notes, 'the walk liberating, I was released from forms, / from the perpendiculars, / straight lines, blocks, boxes, binds / of thought / into the hues, shadings, rises, flowing bends and blends / of sight:'. In many ways, nearly all poetry is a revolt against Platonic forms; if nothing, poetry is an attempt to focus and particularise. And Ammons wants to tell as much as he wants to show. In this poem and in much of the rest of his poetry, Ammons constantly seeks to absorb and witness, and to leave 'things' essentially undisturbed. If nature to Ammons is, indeed 'red in tooth and claw' then Ammons's witness is a fundamental acceptance, 'caught always in the event of change: / a young mottled gull stood free on the shoals / and ate / to vomiting: another gull, squawking possession, cracked a crab, / picked out the entrails, swallowed the soft-shelled legs, a ruddy / turnstone running in to snatch leftover bits:'. Ammons's selection of this scene leans towards the scientific and the objective, but as Harold Bloom comments, what we have here is Ammons's 'oddly negative exuberance'. Which we might allow Ammons, himself, to gloss, with the lines which end 'Corsons Inlet', 'Scope eludes my grasp, that there is no finality of vision, / that I have perceived nothing completely, / that tomorrow is a new walk is a new walk.'

Central to the first volume *Collected Poems 1955–77* is the first of Ammons's book-length sequences, 'Tape for the Turn of the Year', first published in 1965. It was written on one hundred feet of three-inch wide adding machine paper bought, by Ammons's own admission, 'in the House & / Garden store […] to penetrate / into some / fool use for it:' Thus the poem is physically very thin on the page. But that attenuation does not extend to the contents, which include ironic allusions to the *Odyssey*, although the Ithaca Ammons seeks is the Ithaca which houses a job at Cornell. 'Tape for the Turn of the Year' also adumbrates Ammons's search for a phenomenology which can suggest humanity's relationship with the natural world, 'here are "motions" / that play in and out: / unifying / correspondences that / suggest we can approach / unity only by the loss / of things – a loss we're unwilling / to take – / since the gain of unity / would be a vision / of something in the / continuum of nothingness:'. Ammons had lost much in his early life, but seems to be suggesting here that such loss might lead to a greater and more healing unity. It is perhaps this 'unity' which Ammon sees as 'the spiritual which will remain with us as long as we have mind'. If, for Ammons and also for Stevens, God is *Deus Absconditus*, then what might replace that overarching and transcendent unifier is a closer sense of the world.

Ammons continues, 'we already have things: / why fool around: / beer, milk, mushroom cream sauce, / eggs, books, bags, / telephones & rugs: pleasure to perceive / correspondences, facts / that experience is / holding together, that / what mind grew out of / is also holding together:' Although that list of 'things' might seem bathetic, what Ammons seems to be doing is suggesting that humanity might find some of its location in just that sense of the domestic. Ammons has praised the gull cracking open a crab on the shoreline; he is now praising the commonplace products of humanity in the house. In 'Tape for the Turn of the Year', Bloom's 'oddly negative exuberance' is surely turned to a positive exuberance. Ammons wants to sing all of the world of his experience; as Vendler puts it, this is a move from a neo-Platonic One 'in favour of the Many – the vicissitudes of human life', and not only human. It would have been interesting to see how such a sensibility would have reacted to the world of globalisation and social media, with the kind of anomie such 'things' have also created.

Volume two of the *Complete Poems* contains three more book-length sequences: 'Sumerian Vistas', 'Garbage' and 'Glare', as well as individual collections including 'Fucking Right' from 1999, and 'Bosh and Flapdoodle' published posthumously in 2005. Clearly for someone for whom the poetic vocation was of life-long seriousness, Ammons was not without a sense of humour. His short poems continue to plug away at the difficulty of perception, particularly of the natural world; however, Ammons's descriptions of the natural world are, in a sense, a metonym for the perception of anything. Writing of a bush in which a bluejay is singing, Ammons's writes 'and down there / farther where density / hid all but the hermit / lark's song / is a gang of wires, once woodvine'. His structures have moved from the slightly 'open form' and sometimes concrete poetry of the earlier poems, towards a more 'regular' movement of lines in a regular block down the page. The poems are still punctuated with colons, which seem to serve as a catch-all, phrase-, clause- and sentence-marker and allow Ammons to give the illusion that he is writing a poem as a single sentence.

The descriptions in these poems are just as focused and particularised as in the earlier poems, if not more so. And the music of these later poems responds to that particularisation. It is a music that is understated and sometimes quite plain. Often the music is most present when Ammons notates the body in the act of perception, as in, 'but meanwhile my / body knows the wind and / calls it out, / and dust and snow, / the running brook, / praise themselves seen in / my praising sight', this from the poem, 'Vehicle'. Here, the cadences are held in two- or three-stressed, paratactic phrases which run down the page as if to mimic both the wind and the brook. This kind of rhythmic delicacy permeates much of Ammons's poetry of this later period and seems more integrated with the colloquial address which Vendler has pointed out. Dedicated 'to the bacteria, tumblebugs, scavengers, wordsmith – the transfigurers, restorers', 'Garbage' appears to look back on a life absorbed in both domesticities and in success in the poetry business. However, whereas the former might offer a continuing comfort and absorption – early in the poem, Ammons describes soaking soybeans – the latter success, occurs because 'if one succeeds with it one is buttressed by / crowding competitors'. In later life, however, the poet's work continues 'in the poet's mind dead language is hauled / off to and burned down on, the energy held and // shaped into new turns and clusters, the mind / strengthened by what it strengthens'. And the poem continues as a paean to what it means to be *alive* as a poet, sometimes edging towards sentimentality but always held in Ammons's grip by his absorption in what it means to be '"alive" with motion and space'.

Ultimately, Ammons seems to have little traction on the British poetry scene. He has never attracted a British publisher, unlike other American contemporaries, such as W.S. Merwin, C.K. Williams or John Ashbery. In the US, however, Ammons won a range of the premier poetry prizes, including the National Book Award mentioned above, the Wallace Stevens Award from the Academy of American Poets (1998), and a MacArthur Fellowship in 1981, the year the award was established. Harold Bloom edited a volume of essays about Ammons's poetry and there were others, including essays by Geoffrey Hartmann and Donald Davie. These two volumes of his poetry appeared on a number of Best of 2017 lists, which might, perhaps, reignite a waning interest in Ammons in the US, where Ammons was sometimes declared the finest poet of his generation. It is possible that his huge output and his almost single-minded adherence to an Emersonian Transcendentalism has proved off-putting to later readers. If that is the case, it would seem a real pity. It would be a real pity, also, if these two big books simply sat on the shelves in university libraries, as they contain poetry of vast delicacies, great technical resource and huge generosity of spirit.

From the Archive

Issue 141, September–October 2001

SIMON ARMITAGE

From a contribution of two poems, alongside 'The Strid'. Fellow contributors to this issue include Ruth Padel, Neil Astley, Gabriel Josipovici and Roger Scruton.

BIRTHDAY

Bed. Sheets without sleep, and the first birds.
Dawn, at the pace of a yacht.

The first bus, empty, carries its cargo of light
from the depot, like a block of ice.

Dawn, when the mind looks out of its nest,
dawn with gold in its teeth.

In the street, a milk-float moves
by throw of a dice,

the mast to the east raises itself
to its full height. Elsewhere,

someone's husband touches someone's wife.
One day older, the planet weeps. [...]

Three Poems

MARYANN CORBETT

Creed

When I haul my carcass up from my creaking knees
to mumble the old form
(stubbing my tongue on the brick of a new translation)

humble me, Lord, to accept the awkward history
of these your mysteries,
a plotline tangled as the morning news,

a bitterness in the mouth. First, Constantine,
pig-headed in the face of disagreement,
yelling 'Impious fool!'

And Athanasius, wily, on the run,
a glamorous bandit, sending in his thugs
to rile up orthodox riot.

Councils, anathemas, excommunications,
exiles. Seventy years of holy terror,
the violent bearing it away:

a street mob in fourth-century Alexandria
wild with joy at the news
that the Emperor Constantius lay dead,

which left them free to haul out their Arian bishop
and bash him to bloody pulp
to proclaim the Son *homoousios* with the Father.

Yes, in the end they faded away, the Arians –
those pie-eyed optimists, certain
sheer, plodding will could make a man divine –

a lovely notion, dodgy-sounding now
with barbarian tribes at the border
and falling across the empire, shadows of doubt.

Threats

Attention! barks the voice out of the speaker
and once again *Attention!* and our fingers
peck-peck, close documents, log off devices,
grab coats, yank at the bags we schlep our lives in.
A threat has been reported in this building.

Who on this brilliant April day believes it?
Not the last hold-outs, sitting there, still squinting,
peering round-shouldered at the tasks before them.
The voice squawks orders, tinny, razor-edgy.
We file outdoors to our assigned locations.

Was there a warning at the Murrah building?
None. Only the rage of the explosion
monstrously heard at fifty-five miles distant.
That was an April day. The sun was shining,
the wounded building gaping in the daylight.
The children bleeding in the arms of firemen.

But not here, not today. Today, some foul-up –
a fault of wiring? burnt toast in the break room? –
has sprung us, laughing here among pink roses
and petals drifting from the flowering crab trees.

Something could happen, yes. We know things happen.
We have our work, our lives, for the time being.

A Diplomatic Post

After du Bellay, sonnet 86 from Les Regrets

Walk gravely. Keep your brows heavy as lead.
Smile gravely. Fawn; be uber-courteous.
Weigh every word, and nod a sage's head
Balancing *No, my lord,* with *My lord, yes,*

And throwing in a frequent *Ah, just so!*
Add *At you service* – makes you sound sincere.
Expound at length (as if you had a clue)
About the outcome of the current war.

There'll be a lot of hands you have to kiss.
You'll sink a lot of non-existent wealth
Into Italian suits (yes, 'when in Rome...').

And the great thing about a post like this?
Finally, when your wardrobe, luck and health
All fail, they ship you skint and beardless home.

Eight Poems

KRISTÍN ÓMARSDÓTTIR

translated from the Icelandic by Vala Thorodds

waitress in fall

she wipes the blood from her face
(the sword)
rinses the apron in the cold cold water
(in the blue sink)
lays down the apron

the morning dew demands an answer
in order to dry

walks out

*

whether she murdered, was murdered
doesn't matter

*

the autumn air is tender at foothills
clear as water in a truthpond

the morning dew rests
against the blue cheek

Stove

I dreamt I gave you a kitchen stove.
Unearthly and beautiful kitchen stove.
The kitchen stove that everyone dreams of but no one attains.

Its buttons told you everything.
The oven held the deep that no one sees and the bright flames.
The warming drawer was the warming drawer of a winner.

I carried the stove into your room and placed it by the window.
So the taste of the wide expanse and the taste of our isolation would meet

in the pots themselves.

dream

a mother comes back

with an apron round her waist
holds a silent
tray

comes back

pretzels
hot
breadsnails

crawl up

the rim

comes back

golden butter!

her hips clean
her eyes equally blue

comes back

the fragrant luggage

Wool Heart

Though I talk a lot I crave silence about my life.
In the foreground of my life sits you.
To you I bring the words that my life drives away.
And everything I have and all that I have yet to have.
In sleep I live for myself but in waking I live for others.
More rightly said:
In sleep my heart counts down.
In waking my heart is made of wool and there inside I keep your palm.

Tradition

In the shelter of night, men escort women to the hospital.
Whether it's on foot, in a cab, their own car or a borrowed car.
On the lightfaint corridor of the hospital the man sits on a bench or in a chair
while the orderly escorts the woman in to see the doctor.
There the doctor listens to the woman's words and heartbeat.
Or goes into her and takes a test.
Meanwhile the man sits in the corridor and chats to the night guard.
Sometimes the man and the night guard drink coffee from plastic cups but mostly the
    man drinks the coffee from the plastic cup alone.
Before it turns light the door to the examination room opens and the man escorts the
    woman farther down the passages of the hospital.

Morning Gift

The socks are here.

The thread stretches and the thread disappears.
The thread is stubborn and the thread holds nothing.
The thread is blasé and the thread is ablaze.

The socks are here.
I bring them to you with the red dress.

Mood

The nipples of the batteries soften my eyes tonight.
Tonight I will love.
You.

Neglected Knives

The knives in the kitchens of single women who use a lot of food delivery need sharpening desperately. The knives in the knife block are of no use to the bread crust or the proud tomatoes or the patient onion of the woman who accidentally comes with unprepared food into the kitchen of the woman who stops cooking when her lovers disappear.

The impossible knives, their completely impossible knives, neglected and dusty, in intrusive kitchens that only get plugged in if he is nearby who can return the proteins back into the abdomen of the kitchen's owner.

Still, the gardens display their finest. The lemons on the trees await hands that will squeeze them over the old asparagus. And the redcurrant spreads itself over everything like inebriated lanterns though that reminds me mostly of the kisses that we didn't repeat.

And still it is also magnificent to slice vegetables into the stomach of one's love with a sharp knife slice and slice vegetables and again vegetables with a sharp knife into the stomach of one's love slice and slice the vegetables down with a sharp knife. Into the stomach of one's love.

Lovable loveless women, you that open the door to young errand boys who bring you tepid, fertile, plastic containers with food, some in uniform, some in their own clothes but all with the waking young eyes that touch anything in their path, sharpen the knives in your kitchens, sharpen them.

Three Poems

FIONA MOORE

Interruption

Crrrrr crrrrr   crrrrr crrrrr
is a crow ringing is a
telephone hopping blackly across the grass
and you're in my ear saying
is my memory a burden to you?
your voice
matter-of-fact but also concerned
No
this never occurred to me until you
asked (who asked?). It's a fine thing
to live with though I'd rather
live with you. Look over there
on a bench – woman and man
making what they can of each other
and here I am hearing voices
when I'd only expected
to get across the park as fast as possible
through the trees now gone
into their mode of winter,
their growth away slow from their sapling selves
but the shape still visible in them.

Chamber Music

We're at the front on the left and he
he's nearer the stage so I'm looking
looking past his brow and cheek the arc
arc of his skull shadow-hairs outlined
outlined against the light oh to run
run my hand over them and downwards
downwards and press my finger-joints one
one by one to the angle of dark
dark under his ear or to furrow
furrow his throat with my thumb its smooth
smooth electric prickle the slight bump
bump of his Adam's apple and feel
feel him swallow turn his head but no
no after all these thousands of years
years of human development and
and hopelessness I can only sit
sit here hands curled on my lap looking
looking both past and at him wanting
wanting the pianist's score to never
never be turned to the final page

Waking up in a Basement

Even when I feel the stone weight of the house
and the earth of the hill it's built into
I don't really believe in my death,
not even when I sniff the draught that yesterday
was tainted by the smell of a small animal
decaying in the thistles and tangled grass
under the olive trees, whose leaves fall
past the window like elegant rain.
This morning the smell isn't there.
At one time in the past I did, I think,
believe – I certainly lived day after day
in repeatedly unfolding horror.
The sun's come out sideways and is breaking up
orange across the folds of the duvet.
There's a blaze at the corner of my eye
that I need to not look at, partially veiled
though it is by these showers of leaves and
tree-trunks that knot and angle their way skywards.
The bell tower strikes a half-hour.
The evidence of all the deaths it's tolled
is against me: the dead should crowd
my mind, as do the sweet chestnut and pine trees
that cloak this circular chain of hills.
Two shots ring out and the deep valley
moves the noise around: something, perhaps
a deer or wild boar or (heaven forfend) a
small bird may have died now, or be dying –
tasting its own blood amid a sense of
what panic or numb astonishment.

If the Means are Equal

Charles Olson's Reciprocal Exchange

DUNCAN MACKAY

EVEN A CURSORY GLANCE through the *PN Review* archive using the excellent search engine tool on the home page points up clearly how significant to other poets was the American poet Charles Olson, in spite of 'his thought and writing slipping from critical view in the decades following his death in 1970'. The collection of essays under the title *Contemporary Olson* published in 2015 (reviewed in *PN Review* 231, Vol. 43 No. 1, September–October 2016), edited by David Herd, has quickly become a potent reference for contemporary Olson studies, having its international list of contributors. Herd set the agenda as directed to 'where Olson criticism should be looking next'. In a rapidly changing global reality of political and social turbulence, Herd suggested that 'questions of shared vocabularies, of the definition and re-definition of political space, and of individual and collective agency, are firmly back with us'. As a result, Olson's 'thought seems once more a necessary intellectual resource [...] the suppleness and scale with which he is able to figure the complexity of inter-relations (whether between people, between people and the world, or between areas of knowledge) makes him necessary reading in our own politically and economically conflicted moment'. Herd has continued to explore aspects of current social and political turmoil in detail himself through his poetry (*All Just* and *Through*, published by Carcanet in 2012 and 2016 respectively) and in his most recent critical writing, such as his essay 'Valediction Forbidden Mourning: Poetry in the Age of Deportation' in a recent *PN Review* (*PN Review* 235, Volume 43 Number 5, May–June 2017).

Herd's Introduction in *Contemporary Olson* charts Olson's emergence into the vanguard of New American Poetry, identifying the 1950 publication of 'Projective Verse' (written and revised in collaboration with Robert Creeley and Frances Boldereff) as the pivotal moment in the launch of what Olson himself identified as a 'post-modern world'. While 'composition by field' is taken as the central tenet of Olson's projective method (as Herd puts it: 'the metaphor on which all of Olson's innovations hinged'), there is another essential principle that Olson gleaned from physics, integral to the field concept, namely that of 'energy exchange'; a concept without which the better known 'field' is profoundly incomplete. As a conceptual construct gleaned from the nuclear physics of the day, 'energy exchange' functions jointly through both field and particle ontologies, and we might wonder at the degree to which Olson understood (and those of us engaged in literary analysis currently understand) the physics from which he took his analogies.

Both exchange and field notions for the physicist imply an additional 'feedback' concept, which becomes a vital component of Olson's vision for the effectiveness of his writing. However, to begin with the notion of 'energy constructs', it appears early in 'Projective Verse' when Olson considers 'the *kinetics* of the thing' – the dynamics of poem as transducer (that is, as a means of converting one form of energy into another). 'A poem is energy transferred from where the poet got it... by way of the poem itself to, all the way over to, the reader.' As a consequence, 'the poem itself must, at all points, be a high-energy construct and, at all points, an energy-discharge'. In a post-war, rapidly evolving Cold War, circumstance, atomic physics had demonstrated the extraordinary energy content of even the tiniest sub-microscopic 'constructs', encapsulated in Einstein's mass-energy equation, $E=mc$, and released to such devastating effect over Hiroshima and Nagasaki in August 1945. Particle collisions under extreme pressure result in the exchange and release of extraordinary energies. We are familiar today with high energy interactions as probes of matter in such well publicised experiments as those at CERN in Switzerland. The 1930s and '40s had seen comparable experiments but on a much smaller laboratory scale, until in 1952 the first modern particle accelerator (the 'Cosmotron' at Brookhaven on New York's Long Island) began operating.

From one perspective, a particle is no more than a focus of intense energetic potential. Given that analogy, Olson certainly equates poets with research physicists in their use of interactions and exchanges, and their thoughts and poems as exploratory tools. The problem for the poet, of course, is the difficulty of energy transfer between the direct experience and its 'equivalent of the energy which propelled' that experience now expressed in the poem, and then the energetic transfer from poem to reader. In Olson's suggested 'field composition', the principle to be adopted from Robert Creeley is 'form is never more than an extension of content', and the process 'boiled down' to 'one perception must immediately and directly lead to a further perception' (which notion Olson acknowledges he owed to Edward Dahlberg). The process packs in the energy. What are critical are the three successive exchanges: the energy of experience transferred to the poet, then that energy translated by the poet into poem form, and that poem then passing its energy to a reader.

Olson's prose can take a bit of deciphering. His language rarely flows easily and his ideas can seem initially obscure. Nonetheless, as Burt Kimmelman puts it, Olson's 'was the poetry of a hungry intellectual', and his struggle was 'to accommodate new ways of understanding reality that physics especially was dictating' in order to identify 'what relation there can be between [poetic] form and reality'. The extent to which Olson understood the scientific and mathematical ideas is a question we might ask since, according to Kimmelman, these Olson 'may have grasped only in part'. Not that it matters, of course. At least, if it's the creative outcome that matters most, the impetus is of interest but not of overriding significance. However, in so far as Olson is credited with substantive scientific literacy, we better be sure. Peter Middleton, in his recent study of Cold War American poets (*Physics Envy*, published by Chicago University Press in 2015), asserts that 'Olson's leadership in the negotiations between poetry and science was a crucial part of his achievement' and, quoting Robert Creeley, records that much of what was most valuable in Olson's poetics lay in his recognition of the need for a new stance toward the world, a recognition that 'had come primarily from scientific thinking'.

In 'Equal, That Is, to the Real Itself' (Olson's 1957 commentary on a study of Herman Melville), he writes: 'Taking it in [then] towards writing, the discrete, for example, wasn't any longer a good enough base for discourse; and logic (and the sentence as poised on it, a completed thought, in-stead of what it has become, an exchange force) was as loose and inaccurate a system as the body and soul had been, divided from each other and rattling, sticks in a stiff box.' He's arguing that the physical world was no longer exclusively described in terms of separate entities 'rattling about'. Since the discoveries of twentieth-century science show every phenomenon to be part of a contiguous physical reality, 'energy and motion became as important a structure of things as that they are plural, and, by matter, mass'. The pre-Einstein, Newtonian, world of 'classical' physics consisted of objects within the box of absolute time and space linked through gravitational (and by the mid-nineteenth century also electromagnetic) 'forces'. The post-Einstein world prefers a field-like description in which particles as 'energy knots' (as mathematician Herman Weyl, whom we know Olson read, called them in 1949) are an integral part of the space-time field, in a 'continuous' (as opposed to a 'discontinuous') description of the world. The energies exchanged between foci in the physical network are as, if not more, significant than the momentary cohesive knots. At least that's the description, and Olson takes the analogy of the sentence whose energetic exchange content is more important to him than any syntactic self-containment.

Olson's is a somewhat idiosyncratic take on nineteenth- and twentieth-century physics, which did indeed first develop the detailed analysis of energy in thermodynamics and electromagnetism, the latter also having its field development in line with the long-considered gravitational field, but in which the particulate nature of materiality also evolved analytically as an equal partner, for example in the inescapable atomism of chemistry. From Planck's discovery of 1900, the evident quantisation of sub-microscopic matter did nothing to diminish particulate ontologies, and the issue of wave (essentially a field description) versus particle that arose in 1920s quantum physics, offered no easy resolution of the observed dialectic. While general relativity delivered a more effective field description of space-time than the 'classical' particle-and-force picture of the material world, quantum scale physics in practice remained stubbornly particulate even in the face of the subtleties of wave-particle duality and the inescapability of Heisenberg's uncertainty. So

Olson's mid-century take on this is partial. In 'Equal, That Is to the Real Itself', he continues: 'It was even shown that in the infinitely small the older concepts of space ceased to be valid at all.' This is a legitimate assertion of the infinitely small quantum domain in contrast to pre-relativistic concepts of absolute space, saying simply that classical measures of dimension, position, momentum, time or energy are no longer observationally accessible on the smallest scale. To a physicist this will be a perfectly acceptable statement, but Olson's understanding of it seems a little obscure given that he follows it up with the following: 'Quantity – the measurable and numerable – was suddenly as shafted in, to any thing, as it was also, as had been obvious, the striking character of the external world, that all things do extend out.' Ambiguity comes from the word 'shafted'. Is this a metaphorical use of 'arrow-like' implying inclusion or a colloquialism for 'undermined'? If the former, is he saying that everything, however small, *has* quantifiable extension, because that would contradict the immediately preceding sentence, as well as being untrue.

Other evidence shows Olson was well-aware of Heisenberg's uncertainty as at least an observer effect in sub-microscopic scale measurements, so he would surely not make so elementary a mistake. However, if undermined is the sense, it's an oddly complicated way of restating that physical extension is inapplicable at the quantum scale. Is there a muddled thinking here, or merely a misleading complexity of Olsonian convoluted expression? The next sentence is, 'Nothing was now inert fact, all things were there for feeling, to promote it, and be felt; and man, in the midst of it, knowing well how he was folded in, as well as how suddenly and strikingly he could extend himself, spring or, without even moving, go, to far, the farthest – he was suddenly possessed or repossessed of character of being, a thing among things, which I shall call his physicality.' This is definitely one of Olson's more convoluted expressions. He continues: 'It made a re-entry of or to the universe. Reality was without interruption, and we are still in the business of finding out how all action, and thought, have to be refounded.' So a phenomenological assertion of an individual's being part of a 'continuous' natural whole, in itself fair enough and perhaps an evidentially legitimate analogy drawn from the 'subjectivity' Olson observed in quantum physics in contrast to the old distinctions and 'objectivity' of classical physics.

Physics was and is reductionist in nature, and this is particularly true of the particle physics of Olson's day in which the 'building block' (rather than 'field') ontology of atomic, subatomic, nuclear, and all the component varieties of the evolving subject, sought to reduce the observed complexity and multiplicity to the interactions of a few basic entities. Peter Middleton expresses the Olsonian speculation that perhaps a poet working in a parallel enquiry 'might best concentrate on the reduction of complexity to the interactions of a few basic particles, which… might variously be constituents of language, or self, or society'. If so, what does Olson understand by the 'exchange force' idea that he also adopts from particle physics? It says there are particles of matter which are affected by forces such as the electromagnetic force, and there are the exchange particles, literally the 'force carrier' particles, that function between them. Photons, for example, are exchanged when two electrons (both negatively charged) interact. To imagine the repulsive force as an exchanged particle is to imagine the analogy of a ball being thrown from one player to another carrying with it a certain energy (in the form of momentum, which is the product of mass and velocity) which impact we can feel in the 'equal and opposite' reaction of the receiver. The analogy breaks down in trying to envisage the exchange particle carrying an attractive, rather than repulsive, energy, as for example in a proton (positively charge) with electron (negatively charged) interaction, but the principle for the particle physicist remains.

So Olson envisages an exchange of energetic perception-insight-understanding between poet and poem and between poem and reader. The exchange is a speculative relation, an opportunity for interchange, and no longer is a phrase, sentence or poem, to be seen as a separate and 'complete' entity rattling around like a stick in a box. The exchange process is part of that continuity, spatial and temporal, which is Olson's physical and meta-physical ontology. In physics a field description, in contrast to a particle ontology, delineates a 'continuous reality'. For Olson, the present moment is thus a confluence of the many physical fields (spatial and temporal) and various metaphysical field constructs. The field description arises out of a particle ontology. For example, a classical analysis of gravity is defined by Isaac Newton in his 'inverse square' formulation of 1687, which is a macroscopic scale particle representation:

$$F = G \frac{m_1 m_2}{r^2}$$

It asserts that some mysteriously functioning 'force' (F) operates between two identifiable masses (m_1 and m_2) as a function of the square of the distance (r) between them. What evolves out of this is the concept of a 'force field' between the two masses determining the fate of a third object travelling towards one or the other. Drop a ball from any height between Earth and the Moon and 'gravitational force' will pull it towards the more massive and closer object. If you plot incremental positions on its journey, then you can conjure a representation of the continuous force field we imagine delineates the intervening space. This puts a rather pleasing (if presumably unintended) precision on Olson's statement in 'Projective Verse': 'From the moment he ventures into FIELD COMPOSITION [Olson's upper case] – [the poet] put[s] himself in the open – he can go by no track other than the one the poem under hand declares, for itself. Thus he has to behave, and be, instant by instant, aware of... several forces.' Hence, with Olson we have entered a field schema of conceptual imagination, as well as the 'reality' of an Olsonian historical and geographical field with its confluences, in which (to quote him again) 'instant by instant [we expect to be] aware of some [of] several forces'.

Whether electric, magnetic, gravitational or quantum, in a field description of physical reality every point in the field carries a quantity, measurable at least in principle. As a result, whether or not there is a ball in your gravitational field, physicists envisage the field occupying space-time and 'containing' energy as a physical entity – in our example, that would be the gravitational field 'strength'. You may recall photographs of iron filings on a piece of paper above a bar magnetic or perhaps have done the experiment yourself at school. Such a magnetic field made manifest shows not only the distribution of the field as observed in two dimensions, it also shows the relative energetic strength of field at different locations and, since the ball has its own gravitational field just as the Earth and Moon do, albeit much weaker and less extensive, we have an interaction of multiple fields. In fact, for modern physicists, the concept of a multiplicity of vibrating fields is a better description of physical reality than that of interacting 'component' particles. What we see as particles are simply very energetic excitations in the field. You might think of them as temporary 'nodes' arising in a very fine-meshed four-dimensional vibrating space-time net. Particle collisions at CERN are described by physicists as interactions between highly energetic excitations in which the vibration of one is transferred to another: for example, 'energetic proton' excitations generating 'Higgs Boson' excitations. It's the Higgs field that's actually more significant than the localised, temporary, bosons.

In almost any field with its local concentrations of energy, its intensely energetic knots and progressively diminishing energies with distance around those vibrational foci, one can imagine the kinetic relationships, the dynamic interrelationships of vibration, being of a reciprocal nature. Imagine a wave approaching a sloping beach (the wave as a knot or focus). It draws and returns its energy from and to its surroundings, just as its surroundings feed energy into that wave's breaking (through drag) and take it away as the wave dissipates. The focus of energy exchange is governed by the field and the field by the focus. Similarly, the two-dimensional 'rubber-sheet' analogy of popularised General Relativity illustrates a spatial field being distorted by a moving object on it, while the moving object would also itself be steered by curved 2D space were the two-dimensional analogy more realistic than the usual flattened rubber sheet. The recent experimental confirmation of the existence of gravitational waves simply reflects the ongoing distortions of 4D-space-time by the constantly moving masses that are its foci. This also puts an interesting slant on the Creeley-Olson assertion: 'FORM IS NEVER MORE THAN AN EXTENSION OF CONTENT.'

Olson has adopted this reciprocal, feedback notion of energetic knots within an energy field, and the poet going 'by no track other than the one the poem declares for itself' is inescapably governed by that field. The act of making a poem is the poet being moved through that field. The poem itself is an expression of the field: 'every element in an open poem (the syllable, the line, as well as the image, the sound, the sense) must be taken up as participants in the kinetic of the poem just as solidly as we are accustomed to take what we call the objects of reality'. That's 'Projective Verse' again. He goes further: 'The objects which occur at every given moment of composition (of recognition, we can call it) are, can be, must be treated exactly as they do occur therein and not by any ideas of preconceptions outside the poem, must be handled as a series of objects in a field in such a way that a series of tensions (which they also are) are made to *hold*, and to hold exactly inside the content and the context of the poem which has forced itself, through the poet and them, into being'.

Olson seems to have a real feel for physical 'field' dynamics being translated into his discussion of poetics here. The poem and its components, as objects in the field, are energetic constructs with their internal tensions and (as a physicist would describe it) their energetic potentials, to be released only in the exchange process with a reader. Just as a particle's measurable property refers to, indeed defines, its own field, so, as Katherine Hayles puts it, 'any statement in a field model can be made to refer to itself if the statement is part of the field that the model posits; statements have the potential to become self-referential'. In his poem 'The Kingfishers', Olson writes: 'not accumulation but change, the feedback proves, the feedback is / the law'. The 'law' of a field description is that interaction is a continuous feed-back loop: particle to field to particle – just as the energetic photon in the CERN collider vibrationally interacts with the Higgs field which then generates its Higgs boson, while the proton also responds, perhaps converting to a different particle or perhaps by 'self-annihilation'. In the context of a poem such as *Maximus*, every syllable, phrase and breath, is part of the very field it helps define and delineate. The poem subverts any supposition that a speaking subject is separate from the object about which it speaks. The field defines itself. Olson knew from his science that all knowledge is exploratory and provisional; as David Herd puts it 'the consciously incomplete work, the work that understands itself to be in process, is the work that continues to stimulate and enable thought'. Being part of the feedback process that is integral to Olson's field poetics, we, as his readers many years later, remain equally active components in that field.

EGRESS
NEW OPENINGS IN LITERARY ART

DIANE WILLIAMS
KATHRYN SCANLAN
ELEY WILLIAMS
CHRISTINE SCHUTT
GORDON LISH
DAVID HAYDEN
KIMBERLY KING PARSONS
BRIAN EVENSON
SAM LIPSYTE
HOB BROUN
VERONICA SCOTT ESPOSITO

WWW.LITTLEISLANDPRESS.CO.UK/EGRESS

Two Poems

ROBERT MINHINNICK

Boots

He pulls the right one
off, its lace made in some
Vietnamese sweatshop,

fourteen eyelets though he uses only
six, and 200 joule impact
for the steel toecaps,

which must be good he thought
when he saw them years ago
in the Army & Navy, guessing

what it meant, but you don't find those shops
so often now,
and yes they're cracked but not

split and the tongue is
seawater bleached
from those places he walks,

the margins, over limestone
razors, through
pools red with corallina,

difficult because a continent
is drowned here
and a continent begins,

and he has the polish,
a rind left in the tin
of Carr & Day & Martin,

he should take
greater care, and he pulls
the left one off,

always difficult the left,
yes, in greater need,
the left, a mosaic of scars, but the sole

on both sufficient when he
considers the punishment
of the journeys he makes,

the difficult vocabulary
that rock always uses
and him a learner,

always a learner practising
sandstone's syllables, its quartzite
verbs, and he tips the right

and watches a pyramid
of sand build suddenly
and from the left the same,

perfect he thinks, in their way,
and now he smacks
the heels upon the floor,

and then both soles, and there's more
than he ever thought,
those grains collected

on his expeditions
up to the edge, but next
he sweeps that sand away,

dark as violets, white as brass,
and wonders as he knows he must
how much might fill an hourglass?

Ragwort

First time in six
months I unbolt the gate
but still find the lane

locked by brambles
yards across, an
apology of roses.

Smokers' Lane, the kids
call it, where the world
is supposed to happen.

And who are these?
Lovers, I suppose, as if on cue,
he ahead, the horny

tyke, NY ballcap
perched impossibly,
she behind, eyes

to her samsung,
belly pinned by
an iron butterfly,

grass to their waists,
and bored already
or afraid maybe

but resolutely mute
the three of us
as I pick the thorns

out of my jeans –
thorns the size of fingernails –
and they vanish, this pair

through ragwort's
dishclout perfumery,
into their future.

Four Poems

TIM MURDOCH

Ava Gardner in Deia

She knows no shame, but serves to humble
with laughter, a withheld reaction, a glance
or steady quizzical gaze of hopeless sympathy,
pitch-dark eyes glowering, albeit kindly.

She is here to teach, though you imagine that
to be your role, and offer her a poem
personally inscribed, learning to your surprise
she's read it before in your *Penguin Selected*.

Guardians of the Flame

They can tell you an anecdote isn't poetry,
neither other devices – jokes for instance.
Slowly, the list of possibilities diminishes
'til it's impossible to say what you're left with.

Anything you show them they may negate
or offer qualified praise, sending you home
to tinker, temper, adjust, try a bit harder.
Power, whatever that is, hangs in the balance

saying *maybe*, *if*, or *but* – still hesitant
to suggest *what is*, in case that should prove
to be wrong; esoteric thought found wanting;
all the kingdoms of the earth divided.

What do they know? Only the obvious; TT
that vulcanised stone shows its true colours
when dashed by raindrops; that smoke
from olive prunings drifts and plumes lazily

first thing in the morning, then later,
about eleven, when the breeze gets frisky,
spreads in a thin white haze across the *vega*.
What is obvious is open to anyone.

Initiates will argue the toss among themselves,
but close ranks when Candide approaches
with a beaming smile. *Lord Fauntleroy*
they murmur, and hide him under their wing.

By mid-afternoon the air is crystal clear,
the haze has drifted away. Dark mountain ridges
cut a serrated edge through pale blue sky
and tiny sparrows chatter in the pines.

Formentera Dreams

You picture it in yours, as I do in mine,
though you lived there, I never went
and can only imagine the perfect marriage
of a white shoreline and crystal water
sauntering across with articulate fingers,
rubbing the sand into a smooth table top,
inviting the wounded body into play.

Some mornings it was visible from my window,
headland jutting, naked; other times softened,
upholstered in hyalescent platinum mists,
but I never really knew what went on
there – my version was always dramatised,
or distorted with longings, as perhaps
yours is now, peopled with hindsight and regret.

Artesanía

The cement factory is unashamed of itself.
It has work to do: offices, houses, to uphold.

Just because it fringes the turquoise waters
of the western Mediterranean, doesn't mean

it is an unsightly stain on the map, it being
functional, unassuming and almost beautiful;

the sort of down-to-earth, honest installation
to which art professors tend to award prizes.

Picasso's journey started here. Later,
lured by the opulence of La Belle France,

in the pale blue diffidence of her gaze
he would draw himself as her pet monkey

wistfully reconsidering La Malagueña
who once made him proud of his artisan body –

Hephaestos with heavy bones, muscular calves,
bowed legs, the hands of a stone mason.

Snapshot and Image

A Meeting Of Rich And Pound

BARRY WOOD

*Can history show us nothing
but pieces of ourselves, detached,
set to a kind of poetry,
a kind of music, even?* [1]

I

ADRIENNE RICH published her poem-sequence 'Snapshots of a Daughter-in-Law' in the volume of the same name in 1963. The book as a whole – despite some shift in perspective – was written very much in the lyrical, dramatic and narrative styles and modes of her first two books. W. H. Auden had notoriously described the poems in her first book (1951) as 'neatly and modestly dressed' and John Ashbery, even as late as 1966, pigeon-holed her as 'a kind of Emily Dickinson of the suburbs'. Such delimiting judgements are not uncharacteristic of the times, but no less inaccurate; even in her first two books Rich covertly questions such patronising, patriarchal attitudes. The originality of 'Snapshots' is its more direct and uncompromising subversion of masculine conventions of control and oppression and its equally merciless exposure of female complicity in their perpetuation. The sequence was undoubtedly a breakthrough for Rich herself and a significant part of the 1960s revaluation of women's poetry and its relationship to 'the tradition'. Its radicalism was not immediately recognised, in my experience, but its significance was eventually acknowledged even by those with reservations about the work being too programmatic, more propaganda than poetry.

In her 1971 essay 'When We Dead Awaken', Rich speaks of the origins of the sequence, the conditions under which it was written and its importance to her own development and the resurgence of women's writing of which she was a central part. The subtitle of her essay is 'writing as re-vision' and it's clear that she sees 'Snapshots' as a re-visionary work. The essay is part manifesto, part literary autobiography; in one of the autobiographical passages she reveals how the poem was jotted down in fragments and scraps over a period of two years (1958–60) 'during children's naps, brief hours in the library, or at 3:00 a.m. after rising with a wakeful child'. Gradually the fragments began to coalesce under 'a common theme... in a longer, looser mode than I'd trusted myself with before'. The resulting poems were 'directly about experiencing myself as a woman', and reflected that and the concomitant experience of others. The re-visionary mode involved at once a recognition that 'our language has trapped as well as liberated us' and a need 'to know the writing of the past... [overwhelmingly male]... not to pass on a tradition but to break its hold over us'. Rich had reservations about her achievement in 'Snapshots' – 'too literary, too dependent on allusions' – but she nonetheless acknowledges it as a new direction in her work and life. She puts behind her the well-made poem and dedicates herself to a more open and exploratory poetry and poetic. She elaborates this idea in the foreword to *Poems Selected and New 1950–1974* and in a later essay 'Blood, Bread and Poetry: the Location of the Poet' in 1984 in which she stated:

> By 1956 [...] I was finished with the idea of the poem as a single, encapsulated event, a work of art complete in itself; I knew my life was changing, my work was changing, and I needed to indicate [...] my sense of being engaged in a long, continuing process. It seems to me now that this was an oblique political statement – a rejection of the dominant critical idea that the poem's text should be read as separate from the poet's everyday life in the world. It was a declaration that placed poetry in a historical continuity, not above and outside history.

The personal has become the political and any absolute differentiation between the polemical and the poetic is up for grabs.

All this is familiar territory for readers of Rich's poetry. The declarations of independence are important but the origins and originality of her new poetry need not preclude a poetic as well as personal or political provenance for the 'Snapshots' sequence. Acknowledged or unacknowledged, influences are often necessary and occasionally crucial.

Rich herself has always acknowledged – insisted even – that, under the schooling of her father and her university education, male authors were the almost exclusive influences on her development. Donne, Yeats, Frost, Eliot and Auden are frequently mentioned, and Frost and Auden were certainly major influences on her first two books – though there is perhaps the occasional hint of Edna St Vincent Millay. Ezra Pound is cited only in passing and then as a example of the male hegemony rather than as a model. Pound can't be ruled out of the mixture of influences, however, and it's my view that so far as 'Snapshots' is concerned, his influence on the language, tone and structural devices is seminal. On the face of it, the evidence for this is a bit slim: it is not explicitly acknowledged by Rich herself (no *il miglior fabbro*) or by her commentators. But it is compelling because it's difficult to believe that, without the example of Pound's early poetry and particularly *Hugh Selwyn Mauberley*, 'Snapshots' would have emerged from the early morning 'fragments and rough drafts' into the complex statement and structure which Rich eventually created. This is a complicated matter; but the idea of a creative dependence and interaction between works and authors is familiar enough in modernist literature. Would Eliot's 'Prufrock' have existed without the intervention of Laforgue? Or *Mauberley* without Gautier? As opposed to the acknowledged debt to Dickinson in the 1960s or to HD in the 1970s and '80s,[2] Pound is more or less written out of the story of Rich's poetic development, minimised to the point of invisibility. Pound's fascism and anti-Semitism gave every reason for the exclusion, making him part of what she calls in her 1980s sequence 'Contradictions: Tracking Poems' the 'invisible luggage' she barely came into possession of and for decades denied. We're dealing here perhaps with an acute case of the anxiety of influence, a swerving and sublimation which has an ironic but deep and even more complicated indebtedness to her remote and often domineering Jewish father. Rich only began to deal seriously with her relationship with her father in her poetry in the late 1960s and with increasing intensity in essays and poetry in the 1970s and '80s. One troublesome father was enough perhaps.

II

Let me put it this way: there is both a general and a specific case for the connection between 'Snapshots of a Daughter-in-Law' and *Hugh Selwyn Mauberley*. The general case is possibly the less controversial. Both poems were written and published when the authors were in their early/mid-thirties and represented turningpoints in their lives and the direction of their poetry. *Mauberley* has been described as a farewell to London – a personal stocktaking and satirical portrait of the combined aestheticism and commercialisation of English literary culture in the first two decades of the twentieth century. 'Snapshots' presents a similar breakaway, in which Rich consciously forged a new style and structure and distanced herself from the social and literary traditions she had so far adhered to. Both works are discontinuous in form – poem-sequences which cohere loosely around a common theme, and exploit an instability of persona with ambivalent and sometimes confusing effect. The poems make frequent use of allusion and what Kenner calls 'the poetry of quotation' and are thus thoroughly 'literary' poems. But their literariness is precisely the point: both take facets of the world of literature to represent the broader culture and society. Both sequences cultivate clarity, hardness and an ironical distance between speaker and object. In addition to being deeply personal both are often savagely satirical. And both poems constitute a prelude to change and liberation. For Rich, the task is to shift the perception of the whole burden of a male-dominated tradition and create the possibility of an alternative; for Pound – an easier task perhaps – it is to unmask a decadent, self-defeating and destructive political and cultural 'botch'. Both have their work cut out for them, to adapt a phrase from the end of Rich's 'When We Dead Awaken' essay.

So far, so good. Yet the only direct reference to the broad similarities between the two works which I've found is a rather dismissive suggestion that the 'discontinuity' of method in 'Snapshots' is down to Pound and is responsible for the 'limitation and failure' of Rich's poem.[3] This is a skewed argument driven more by ideology than analysis and itself fails to recognise the consummate craft and originality of Rich's poem and Pound's example. In each case the originality goes along with a powerful emotional commitment. Anyone who has heard Pound's reading of the anti-war sections of *Mauberley* will be in no doubt about the anger and ironical disdain for English imperialist culture in the 1910s; and a similar anger and dark humour is evident in Rich's sequence: 'Sometimes she's let the tapstream scald her arm, / a match burn to her thumbnail, // or held her hand above the kettle's snout / right in the woolly steam'. Pound's poem is one of rejection and scorn and Rich's one of anguished and bitter recrimination and rebellion. They match each other blow for blow and their targets are not that dissimilar: a complacent and repressive culture.

The general links have, in my reading, a more specific basis. Poem five of 'Snapshots' is my starting point:

Dulce ridens, dulce loquens,
she shaves her legs until they gleam
like petrified mammoth-tusk.

The poem starts with a variant on a line in Horace: Odes I:xxii: '*dulce ridentem Lalagen amabo / dulce loquentem*' which James Michie translates as: 'I'll still love Lalage, my sweet / Chatterer with the charming voice'. The epigrammatic version used by Rich succinctly encapsulates this masculine idea of feminine grace and beauty and immediately subverts it with the sharp imagery of the following lines. The poem uses a device characteristic of the sequence where a quotation is directly countered in the subsequent verses. It is a device used for similar purposes by Pound in his imagist and epigrammatic poems of 'Lustra' and 'Cathay'. (The line also echoes Horace's '*dulce et decorum*' phrase used by Pound in *Mauberley*: IV.) Rich's verses don't follow the strict five-seven-five pattern of the haiku, but it is an imagist poem after the fashion Pound learned from Fenellosa. It is the first clear indication that in the shadows at the back of Rich's poem there lurks the 'troublesome' spirit of EP.

These three lines also mark a pivotal moment in the sequence – the point at which the bitter and angry tone of the first four poems – 'all the old knives / that have rusted in my back, I drive in yours, / *ma semblable, ma soeur!*' – switches to the ironic dismantling of the masculine attitudes to women in the tradition in which 'men wrote poems and women inhabited them'. The target for the satire in the first four poems is a matriarchal culture within which women are imprisoned as much by their own complicity as by the oppressive patriarchy. The entrapment is expressed with a fierce irony and pathos in poem four, a snapshot of Emily Dickinson writing '*My Life had stood – a Loaded Gun –* / in that Amherst pantry while the jellies boil and scum'. Rich contextualises and revives the shock of Dickinson's image and charges it with an even more incisive bitterness in those boiling jellies and scum. (Rich returns to this disjunction of images – the explosive and the domestic – in her superb essay on Dickinson: 'Vesuvius at Home'.)

Poem five is the only one of the sequence which approximates the Imagist form; but 1–4 and perhaps more so 6–9 can be seen as translating into something like Pound's ideogram, his elaboration of the short imagist poem into a larger intellectual and emotional complex. The snapshots open out into broader cultural and historical pictures and perspectives. The Poundian influence is evident not only in the Imagist/ideogrammatic device but also in the ironical tone of the poems which, for the most part, target the complacent masculine culture by quoting, challenging and resisting it. The tone is certainly not unlike that of Pound's early urban poems such as 'The Garden' and the satirical verses in 'Moeurs Contemporaines'. This is well exemplified in poem nine of 'Snapshots' where we are told 'Time is male' and that any attempt to 'smash the mold' brings on 'solitary confinement, / tear-gas, attrition shelling'. The poem ends with a cautionary aside: 'Few candidates for that honour', an echo of the Poundian manner in which he is at once appropriated and displaced. Stealing the language: what better way to dispel the ghost than to pinch his style?

Poem ten of the sequence continues the ironic tone of poem nine – 'Well, / she's long about her coming' – but the form is more photomontage than snapshot or ideogram, a series of fragments, only partially conjoined, which recall the end of *The Waste Land* rather than the more decisive act of closure in *Mauberley*. The last three words of Rich's poem: 'delivered / palpable / ours' offer a promise rather than fulfilment, an anticipatory chant or prayer rather than an arrival. 'My soul, my helicopter', as she puts it in the wonderful poem 'In the Woods' (1963) still has some way to go before it realises itself – body, intellect and imagination running together. In the volumes and in the increasing number of poem-sequences which succeed 'Snapshots'; in the extraordinary group of Dickinson-inspired poems in *Necessities of Life* (1966), in 'The Phenomenology of Anger' (1972) and in 'From an Old House in America' (1974) Rich is still engaged with 'breaking away' from the biological and literary fathers and the enclosing tolerance of and oppression by the patriarchal traditions. The realisation of the 'promise' proposed in 'Snapshots' finally arrives: 'delivered / palpable / ours' in *The Dream of a Common Language* (1978), particularly in 'Twenty-One Love Poems' – in which Robert Lowell is appropriated and banished – and the magnificent 'Transcendental Etude' which envisages a paradisal fulfilment 'not somewhere else but here'. The poem is in the tradition of great Romantic and modern meditations which Rich has in effect reinvented: 'Tintern Abbey', 'Ode to Autumn', Eliot's 'Little Gidding', Stevens's 'Sunday Morning' and Bishop's 'At the Fish Houses' and 'The Moose'. Pound's Dantean dream never, as he admitted, cohered in this way; it wasn't until he was put in a cage outside Pisa that he was able (almost) to write himself out of madness and nightmare.

Another poem-sequence in *The Dream of a Common Language* is, for my purposes, notable for the fact that it is the only instance I can find of Rich quoting Pound directly. The poems in 'Natural Resources' are written in unrhymed couplets which Rich seems to have adopted from the later work of HD, although they may also draw on her enthusiasm for the ghazals of Mirza Ghalib. The poem is an exploration of the difficult relationships between women and men, pursued with an often caustic wit (see the dialogue poem four) and an understanding of the need to 'reconstitute' the world so that such conflicts and wearisome antagonisms are no longer necessary. In a central section of the sequence Rich imagines 'a fellow creature / with natural resources equal to our own', but follows up in the next section with the image 'of another kind of being... // – a mutant, some have said: the blood-compelled exemplar / of a 'botched civilisation' / as one of them called it // children picking up guns / for that is what it means to be a man'. The phrase from Pound's anti-war poem five in *Hugh Selwyn Mauberley* is another example of how Rich draws attention to Pound whilst diminishing his status to 'one of them'. It is also part-recognition that the hope for the radical reconstitution of the world is faint and that nothing will change when the violent male-dominated world continues to require 'women's blood for life / a woman's breast to lay its nightmares on'. The poem is polemical but nonetheless, for a male reader, discomforting; for the poet herself, a decade after 'Snapshots', it represents a frustration, close to despair, that her work is still to do. The sequence also makes a wry, passing allusion to Whitman's 'noiseless patient spider'.

III

The imagist poem at the heart of 'Snapshots', the ironic tone and use of allusion in the sequence as a whole, the ideogram form of individual poems and the fragmentary structure of the sequence may not be conclusive proof of the Poundian provenance of Rich's work. But the possibility of a connection is intriguing and in my experience enriches the reading of both works. The uniqueness of a literary work is not compromised or diminished by its debt to other works and authors; on the contrary, it will often be necessary to its originality. Again, the direct quotation from *Mauberley* in another poem-sequence written and published two decades after 'Snapshots' is not proof of the possibility of creative dialogue; but Rich, like Pound, is a poet of great self-consciousness and consciousness of the power of literary traditions. It seems unlikely that the reference to a 'botched civilisation' is there by accident rather than with deliberate and even mischievous intent.

There are two other tangential and politically weighted links which, whilst somewhat speculative, suggest the possibility of an early and continuing interest in Pound even though he was certainly a poet and man whom Rich would have found intolerable and abhorrent. When Pound was awarded the Bollingen Prize for *The Pisan Cantos* in 1949, shortly after his incarceration in St Elizabeth's Mental Asylum in Washington to escape trial for treason, Rich was a student at Radcliffe. Well and widely read, it seems inconceivable that she wasn't aware of the scandal and controversy surrounding the award. And later in 1983, in a review of Elizabeth Bishop's *Complete Poems 1927–1979*, she makes a point of commenting on Bishop's 'Visits to St Elizabeth's' as 'a seriously political poem'.

> I'm beginning to feel like Whitman's spider launching forth filament after filament until the gossamer thread catches and makes good the argument. Still, it's worth pursuing one further aspect of this curious entanglement of Rich and Pound.

After 'Snapshots' and after *Mauberley*, Rich and Pound launch themselves into more ambitious projects – in Pound's phrase, long poems including history. In Rich's case the poet/daughter-in-law is translated into the poet-bard – speaking for more than herself – and although she reorientates herself towards her female lineage – Bradstreet, Bronte, Dickinson, HD – she also takes on, on her own terms, the legacy of Whitman and some of his twentieth-century followers such as Jeffers, Olson and even Pound. From *The Dream of a Common Language* (1978) through to *Dark Fields of the Republic* (1996), Rich is engaged with an epic endeavour – a long poem which in particular sees contemporary American history and the modern history of Jewish culture and emigration within the complex of her own personal history as poet, essayist and activist. The project is not unlike Pound's transformation from literary provocateur in the London years to the poet who saw himself as the inheritor of the epic destiny of Homer, Dante and his 'pig-headed' father Walt Whitman. Both poets were great essayists and in their essays they are often polemical, provocative, even dogmatic; but their poetry, while not without polemicism and provocations, is at its best when it does what we tend to think poetry should do and engages in a constantly evolving relationship with the reader and with the complexities of experience and history. Rich articulates this conception of the truth of poetry in 'Contradictions: Tracking Poems', another poem-sequence which ends (though without a full-stop):

> You for whom I write this
> in the night hours when the wrecked cartilage
> sifts round the mystical jointure of the bones
> when the insect of the detritus crawls
> from shoulder to elbow to wristbone
> remember   the body's pain and the pain on the streets
> are not the same   but you can learn
> from the edges that blur   O you who love clear edges
> more than anything   watch the edges that blur

This has a sureness of touch and feeling, which Pound too occasionally achieves in some passages of *The Pisan Cantos*.

By the late 1970s, and throughout the 1980s and '90s, Rich had certainly given up, as she declared in 1975, the poem as 'a single, encapsulated event' in favour of poetry as 'a long continuous process'. Just as Walt Whitman gathered his life's work under the title of *Leaves of Grass* and Pound called his ongoing epic *The Cantos*, it would seem appropriate for Rich's later work to be gathered under a collective and inclusive title: *The Dream of a Common Language* perhaps.

Notes

1 Adrienne Cecil Rich 'Readings of History' Phi Beta Kappa poem, William and Mary College, 1960. I first read this poem-sequence in Donald Hall, *Contemporary American Poetry* (1962). I was particularly struck by what I now think of as the imagist lines: 'Today, a fresh clean morning. / Your camera stabs me unawares, / right in my mortal part'. The poem was published in *Snapshots of a Daughter-in-Law* (1963) but excluded from later selected poems and only reappeared in *Collected Poems 1950–2012* (2016).
2 Hilda Doolittle: Pound assigned the literary sobriquet 'HD, Imagiste' in 1912.
3 Cheryl Spector, *Encyclopedia of American Poetry: 20th Century*, 1986.

*

Postscript

I am writing this during the summer of 2017 when the president of the United States has signed an order to prevent transgender people from serving in the US military forces, has engaged in a joust with his companion in folly the president of North Korea and has stirred up and endorsed racism and anti-Semitism in the American heartland to a degree not seen since the days of the Goldwater campaign. It occurs to me Pound's politics and political behaviour of the 1930s and '40s had more than a whiff of Trumpism about it and appealed to a pathology in American culture and society – ranging from a peculiar naivety to outright viciousness – which needs to be analysed and understood in order to be comprehensibly challenged and rebutted. As an admirer for more than fifty years of what William Carlos Williams called, with irony, 'the pure products of America', and as a constant if frequently dismayed reader of Pound's work, now seems an appropriate moment to become reacquainted with the deep dark roots of America's contradictions and confusions.

A study of Pound may not be the most straightforward way of engaging with these issues, but it could be an illuminating one. Equally now is certainly a good time to return to the sanity, generosity and complexity of Adrienne Rich's investigations of the 'dark fields of the Republic'.

A salutary starting point might be her Brechtian poem 'What Kind of Times Are These' (1991), which opens with an idyll of the American landscape, 'a place between two stands of trees where grass grows uphill', and ends:

> I won't tell you where the place is, the dark mesh of the woods
> meeting the unmarked strip of light –
> ghost-ridden crossroads, leafmold paradise:
> I know already who wants to buy it, sell it, make it disappear.
>
> And I won't tell you where it is, so why do I tell you
> anything? Because you still listen, because in times like these
> to have you listen at all, it's necessary
> to talk about trees.

Four Poems

ASHLEY ANNA MCHUGH

On the Death of Alexander

after 'Aristotle with a Bust of Homer' by Rembrandt

Here is the emblem of my Grecian king
who went beyond the reaches of the west,
who took what caught his eye
        then burnt the rest –
not caring that was nearly everything.

I gave him what I could – small offering,
this patterned way of thought.
        He beat his chest.
He knew already. He was unimpressed.
I'd wanted him to hear the muses sing –

but he only saw the heroes in your story,
triumphant and clever. Not the wine-dark sea.
Carved now in stone, great poet, sing to me
about the enduring bitterness of glory –

grand symphonies, distilled to a single tone.
How what survives of us, survives alone.

The Doctor Asks If I Was Abused

Not all kissed bruises. Not all milk and cake.
Look, even though I was a child once,
I couldn't tell you now what it was like

but I can tell you what it's not, a snake
that gossips in a circle under the fence.
Not all kissed bruises. Not all milk and cake.

Not all hard work, but not a game of luck –
although I saw some luck, before and since.
I couldn't tell you now what it was like:

My bloody fingerprint by a sun-struck lake –
or the fishhook gleaming as it pierced my skin.
Not all kissed bruises. Not all milk and cake.

Quick as a match, the violent scratch and strike –
my flame blown out. I only needed a chance.
I couldn't tell you now what it was like

but no, I won't go back there. Just you look –
that vase will never bloom. No backward glance,
no bruises. Give your children milk and cake
and kiss their faces. Tell me what it's like.

Chasing the Cosmos

Gigantic and cold, the harvest moon at dusk
seems certain – her loneliness is all I need.
But I'm thinking of you:
        Of planting a single seed,
knuckle-deep – and imagining your husk
split open. How I always wanted you,
your lush leaves bright beside a heavy bloom.
How many nights I dreamed of that perfume.
How nothing grew.
        Bad seed, you always knew
I'd claw you out barehanded. Dead as stone.

Lie still and watch as the tipsy starlight turns
around the moon –
        I want to learn to love
this world like she does, circling high above
its distant darkness – but rising on her own.

How even halved by its shadow, she still burns.

The Leap

for David & Catherine

I

You sometimes saw her with a cigarette
up on the rooftop, pacing late at night,
always alone. You say she rarely talked,
and smiled like a hook had gotten caught
in the corner of her mouth, quick jerk of the line
before she looked away. You say her laugh
was like an empty beer can clattering
across the asphalt – a thin, metallic sound –
and that she'd bend to crush her cherry out,
no matter how much longer it would burn,
whenever you approached her in the dark.
You thought she wanted to be left alone,
and started smoking by the loading dock.

She leapt from our rooftop, eighteen stories up,
the full pill bottles still on her bathroom sink.

How could you have known? You couldn't know,
I tell you – but I know you don't believe me,
and I doubt you ever will – one reason why

I love you, how you hold the world so close
against your heart, a wounded bird you found
in the city park one summer as a boy –
and how you used your shirt to swaddle it
and carried it back home, how carefully
you built a nest inside a cardboard box
and laid it there to rest – and how you slept
beside it in your sleeping bag, but woke
to clouded eyes and rigid wings, the way
you dug its grave and covered it with bricks,
then told your sister it had flown away.

I love not just this story, but the way
you told it – solemnly, voice soft and strained –
as though it were a secret no one knew,
the quiet way you cradle what you love.

II

Our windows open to the summer heat,
you pour another glass of wine for me –
the last of its kind, the bottle empty now,
and then you kiss my forehead as you leave
to get yourself more gin – a little drunk
and halting, back when I was young, I say,
there was a new professor I admired
and in his office, talking after hours,
he gestured at the books surrounding us,
then built a stack he wanted me to read.

Most first editions, some of them were signed –
a few were filled with his handwritten notes.

Of course, I didn't know that at the time.
He told me that he didn't need them back.

He must have known already he was dying.

I never guessed – it didn't cross my mind –
but by the spring semester, he was gone.
He gave me all those books, and even now,
there are so many left that I haven't read –
his last name penciled on the title page.
I think – I've let him down, I say. But you
don't answer right away. I look outside,
and the sun is going down across the river.
I know you're thinking of the girl who died.

III

Nothing left to say, my mind goes back
to when I lived in Boston, long years spent
commuting to the city – not quite dawn,
the lace of winter laid on unlit windows,
snow wisping like a skirt of white organza,
drifting along the pavement with the wind –
walking in silence through a muffled world.

I was alone – but at that early hour,
it seemed like everybody else was, too.

We waited for the train in silence, crowds
gathered together on the subway platform,
shoulders jostling shoulders on the train.
We hurried on the sidewalks, side by side,
and never spoke. Polite and perfect silence.

But now, I only think of how I stood
surrounded by those strangers in the fog
beside the station. How they must have been
the same two dozen people every day.

How long we waited in that dark unknowing,
each looking for some nearly empty train
to carry us away – but we never spoke.
Just listened to the automated voice recite,
Stand clear of the closing doors. How, even now,
eyes closed, I still can't see a single face

except my own, distorted in the glass –
the only gaze that follows me alone.

Allen Present & Absent[1]

C.K. STEAD

EARLY IN HIS BIOGRAPHY, before he's really discussed many of Curnow's adult friendships, Terry Sturm writes this:

> [Curnow's] great preference (and need) was for close, trusted personal friendships, and there were not a great many of these in his life: Glover, Lilburn from this time on, and later his brother Tony and W. H. (Bill) Pearson, his colleague at the University of Auckland. He could always talk and write to these without reserve, assured that whatever confidences he revealed would be respected, and his loyalty to them in turn throughout his life was absolute. His relationship with Karl Stead, later, was more complex. It was primarily a literary relationship, based on Curnow's side on unstinting respect for the quality of Stead's literary judgements, but there was always an element of reserve in personal matters, a sense (perhaps unfair since Stead's letters to Curnow were always open and direct) of never being quite sure what confidences might not be turned against him.

There's no reference for this. It doesn't sound to me in the least like anything Allen would have said – it's not his *style*. It comes, I'm sure, from his widow, Jeny, who had written her own unpublished biography of Allen. It may even be true. I don't think so; but if it is, the way it's expressed here isn't right. If there was uneasiness about me, I think it would have been about what Allen called my tendency to 'candour'. (He may have meant reckless candour.) What, after all, were the little secrets that were not made known to me so that they should not be publically disclosed? I felt I knew most of Allen and Jeny's secrets, and that most of the literary world did too, and 'disclosure' would hardly have been worth the bother or constituted a scoop.

But I cite this as an example of something I feel about the book as a whole: that it has been written with the widow looking over the author's shoulder. Terry Sturm is scrupulous: in this example he puts down what he's told, but then worries about it, and adds that parenthesis – 'perhaps unfair because Stead's letters...' etc.

Does the book 'catch' Curnow? Yes and no. There was always an aspect of Allen I thought of as the larrikin-radical (Dennis Glover's best mate) and it is absent here. Other qualities too are missing, but I'll stick to this one for the moment and try to give you an idea of what I mean.

I've written in *South-West of Eden* about my student experience of Curnow and I won't repeat any of that; but I'll jump forward to late 1959 (when I came back from four years away from New Zealand) through to March 1961 when Allen went off on his first sabbatical.

The personal interchanges with Curnow during that period were intense and exhausting. He was in a state of quite extreme agitation – much more extreme than you would guess from the biography. There were his troubles with the Wellington poets who were obstructing the publication of his Penguin anthology of New Zealand verse. But even more agitating, it seemed, was the fact that his play, *Moon Section*, had been panned in the local papers and had failed commercially. Allen needed a sympathetic ear, which mine was – always; but I was myself in a state of anxiety, preparing lectures on subjects I'd never taught before, and with an unfinished PhD thesis still hanging over me. I was skinny with the effort and angst of it all, too busy to stop and talk to anyone, and yet there was no respectful escape from Allen's pained, unstoppable monologues. I told [my wife] Kay he was my Ancient Mariner, and I would report after one of our encounters that I'd been 'Marinered' again.

1960 was the year when I was to give one of a series of Winter Lectures on the theme of New Zealand's 'remoteness'. The lecturers chosen were a distinguished lot: Keith Sinclair on History, R. McD. Chapman on Politics, Eric McCormick on Society, Jack Golson on Anthropology, Andrew Sharp (the earlier one) on Polynesian voyaging. My contribution was to be on our literature, and for a newly appointed lecturer it was a great honour to be included. It was my first ever public lecture. Allen knew I was terrified, and although I had given him no indication of what I was going to say, he gave me support and encouragement. He was there in a side room with me before I went 'over the top'; and he was there in the audience to hear it and to join the applause.

That lecture put Curnow right at the centre of New Zealand's literary situation, and how it could be seen to be affected by our 'remoteness'. It began by quoting his lines:

> Wholehearted he can't move
> From where he is, nor love
>
> Whole hearted that place...

It took issue with the James K. Baxter, Louis Johnson, Alistair Campbell group (and also my fellow lecturers Sinclair and Chapman) who were challenging Curnow's authority as anthologist and what they were calling his 'South Island myth'; it argued that his was 'an achievement quite unequalled by any other New Zealand poet'; and it ended with a quotation from Curnow's poem, 'When the hulk of the world', which made the point about 'remoteness' and gave my lecture its title.

Sturm calls 'When the hulk of the world' 'one of the most intense love poems Curnow ever wrote'. He traces its genesis to an affair during Curnow's first overseas visit in 1949–50, about which of course I knew nothing; and he subjects it to two or three pages of close reading. I didn't analyse it. I simply kept it until last, and then hit the audience with its full force – a way of winding up the lecture to demonstrate how much 'remoteness' did affect us, how deeply it was felt in that time when sea travel was the norm and put four and half to five weeks between us and Europe, and when there was no internet, no e-mail, no instant communication; all of that, and how Curnow at his rhetorical best could rise to it, make it felt, make you feel it:

> Seas will be seas, the same;
> Thick as our blood may flood our opposite isles
> Chase each other round till the quiet poles
>   Crack, and the six-day top
> Totter, but catch us neither sight nor hold;
> Place will be place, limbs may not fold
>   Their natural death in dreams.
> I pray, pray for me on some spring-wet pavement
> Where halts the heartprint of our salt bereavement,
>   Pray over many times,
> Forgive him the seas, forgive him the spring leaf
> All bloom ungathered perishable as grief
>   For the hulk of the world's between.

The lecture was a great success. Sturm doesn't mention it – strange, because I know how important it was to Allen, particularly because he'd begun to feel, as writers often do in their late forties, that a younger generation was breathing down his neck and hoping to replace him. The fact that I was ten years younger again than the ones who were opposing him was important.

At some time during that same year there was an occasion when the Curnows (Allen and his first wife Betty) and the Steads were at a party together on the town side, I think at the Lowrys', and Kay and I drove them home across the new harbour bridge in our little Ford Popular. Allen invited us in for a nightcap, as you did in those days; and then he thought of the bantams that roosted in their macrocarpa, and said he and I should go out and swing on the branches and 'shake them up' – or down. Many years later I put it into a very literary sonnet about Auckland's North Shore as an enclave of writers, which began with an echo of *Macbeth* and ended with an echo of the lines from *Henry IV* (I) which are on Katherine Mansfield's grave (the ones quoted by Neville Chamberlain before his Munich meeting with Hitler):

> To Maurice and to Maurice and to Maurice
> Duggan, Shadbolt, Gee, how they load us down with fictions
>
> And all our yesterdays maybe have lighted fools
> The way to Dostoyevski. How many years ago was it
>
> That Curnow's bantams roosted in his macrocarpa,
> And he and I one midnight crept under the moon
>
> And swung on the branches bringing those feathered half-wits
> Down around our head with a flapping and a squawking
>
> That echoed over Big Shoal Bay. Do good poets
> Make bad professors? Do many Maurices
>
> Make light work, as one Sargeson made a Summer?
> How many K. S's could the North Shore harbour
>
> Before the Fall? I tell you my Lord Fool
> Out of these nettle prophets we still pluck our safety pins.

For me this bantam-shaking was a significant moment, revealing an aspect of the man that was always there somewhere just below the surface. It was Curnow *ludens*, the comic spirit that would be let loose much later in poems like 'Organo et Libitum' and the Raynor poem, 'A Fellow Being'. That Curnow would never be entirely absent from the poems; but it was to be gradually edited out of the public face. As time went on his behaviour became impeccable: no more shaking of sleeping bantams out of trees.

In December of that year the Curnow daughter Belinda was married and Kay and I were back at Herbert Street for the wedding.

The following March Allen left on his first sabbatical after ten years in the job, and Kay and I were there on the wharf with Betty to wave him away. Possibly we'd driven them there. It was that extraordinary ritual of farewell at the wharf-side that counted for so much in those days, when travelling 'overseas' was rare and dramatically significant; with the ritual streamers stretching from sea-to-shore; and then the final shuddering blast of the horn that signalled the ship was moving – and the streamers stretched and finally broke, and the two sets of human faces were slowly lost to one another.

What was odd on this occasion was that once we'd seen Allen on board and arranged ourselves with our streamers in the crowd on the wharf, with Allen up there at the rail waving, it became apparent that he was waving to us and then vanishing; clearly somewhere in the crowd at another point along the wharf there was another he was farewelling. Kay and I had known about the 'other', Jeny Tole; and as long ago as 1955, when I was an MA student, Betty had told me that she knew Allen 'had a mistress'; so I supposed she was guessing, as we were, that 'the mistress' was the other person being farewelled. But she said nothing about it; and neither did we. She just said she was worried that Allen might not have a change of underclothes. The Sturm biography reveals that Betty was hoping this leave would bring about a severance with 'the mistress'. What she didn't know, and neither did we, was that Allen was saying goodbye to her forever. He was planning to do what T. S. Eliot had done in 1933–34 when he used a lecture tour in the United States to effect a separation from his wife Vivien, and then while away wrote to tell her he would not be back.

When we next saw Allen he was living in what he characteristically called 'a mothel' in Grafton Road, preserving the necessary distances preliminary to divorce proceedings.

*

Now I want to move on to 1964, when I was promoted to Associate Professor and Bill Pearson and Allen were not. I was ten years younger than Bill, twenty years younger than Allen. Bill was upset, Allen was hurt, and Terry quotes what he wrote to Bill about it: it was a rat race, Allen said, 'one for which Karl has been in rigorous training both tactically and intellectually'. I had of course, he was right. The training had recently produced a book called *The New Poetic* – in later incarnations *The New Poetic: Yeats to Eliot*; and also, a substantial article in *Landfall* called 'Allen Curnow's poetry', which on page three hundred and ninety-four, just two pages before we come to the promotion crux, Sturm calls 'brilliant', 'deeply influential on subsequent understanding' of Curnow, 'seminal', 'persuasive in depth and detail' – and so on.

Promotions were not on a quota system. If I had not had mine Allen would not therefore have had his – and I'm sure he must have known that. What my promotion meant was that I was soon elected to the Promotions Advisory Committee, and was able, first, to warn Curnow to change one of his referees who was doing no good at all to his chances, and second to argue in his favour on the committee – otherwise I can say he would never have got the promotion to associate professor that came in 1966 or '67. But here's what Sturm writes about the outcome of all this on page three hundred and ninety-six: 'For the remainder of his time at the university [that is from 1964 to 1975] Curnow retained a certain reserve in his personal relations with Stead.'

That's eleven years' cold shoulder! That was the decade during which Allen and Jeny moved into our little house in Maunsell Road when we moved out of it and bought in Tohunga Crescent; and in 1965 when we were away on leave and they married, they bought the house across the road from us. Later, when they went on leave, they lent us their bach on Lone Kauri Road and we bought a section there and built a bach of our own. There was endless cross-crescent commerce during those years – dinner parties, parties, literary gossip, intimate conversations (all still as yet publicly 'undisclosed'!); and, of course, it accelerated and changed focus towards the end of this period when he began to write new poems and to seek my opinion on them. Somehow this cold shoulder went unnoticed. Neither Kay nor I can remember it.

But there was an issue between Allen and me. It came actually *after* this period, and it's one I think Sturm deals with well. This was my public lecture at the Wellington Writer's Festival in 1979, a piece of revisionist NZ Lit Hist in which I suggested it might be time to change the terms in which New Zealand poetry was discussed, from Curnow's essentially nationalist ones ('the New Zealand thing, the regional thing, the real thing' as he called it once, or just 'the New Zealand referent') and think instead about the larger developments in poetry in the Anglophone world and see how our poetry looked from that perspective.

This involved a piece of literary history for which I was well equipped because I was just at that time close to finishing what was to be my last academic study of twentieth-century poetry in English.[2] So I saw Curnow and his generation as products of what I called 'Modern' poetry in the twentieth century, where the prime debt was to British Auden and his cohort, and to the Georgians before them; and the Ian Wedde generation as Modernists, whose debt was to Americans Ezra Pound and William Carlos Williams. And all this was neatly illustrated by the fact that Allen had called his son Wystan, and Wedde had called his son Carlos – Wystan Auden and Carlos Williams, the progenitor in each case. I characterised these two schools as 'closed' – the Moderns, in that they used closed poetic forms – and 'open' – the Modernists who tended to sprawl and let the poem's internal pressures dictate shape and form.

It was neat enough, persuasive up to a point; but Lit Hist is a crude instrument. It deals in broad categories – Jacobeans, Metaphysicals, Augustans, Romantics, Aesthetes, Georgians, 'the Movement', Modernism. These are serviceable categories, especially after the time has passed; but it ignores how most poets dislike being fitted into schools and categories. Wedde was no happier about it than Allen was; and it troubled Allen especially that I pointed out there had been a gap in his production of new poems that had lasted almost twelve years. I never quite understood why this was such a sensitive point, because it seemed to me to illustrate the authenticity of his work. To use an Auden phrase, Allen was being 'lived by history'. There had been that gap in his work while in some interior way he was absorbing what history required of him. When he emerged from that silence, the new poems were 'something different, something nobody counted on', least of all Curnow himself. As the famous Pound dictum required, he had 'made it new'. It's still an interesting, and maybe even a serviceable, idea – one I liked to entertain without believing everything was finally and definitively explained by it. Of course, if the silence had gone on I would never have referred to it; but it seemed to have ended triumphantly, and I was trying to celebrate it, and the new work it had made possible.

Actually from Allen's point of view it could have been much worse. As I thought about all this there had been a novel I might write brewing up, a very Henry Jamesian idea, of an older poet (this was thinking of Curnow and James K. Baxter) who fell silent as a brilliant younger practitioner took all the public attention; and who then came roaring back into full poetic life when the younger poet died. Baxter died, aged forty-six in 1972, the year that marked Curnow's resurgence. Fortunately for good cross-Crescent relations there was another idea for a novel that seemed even more attractive. It was based on our (Kay's and my) experiences with Frank Sargeson and Janet Frame in 1955. I moved it back in time to 1951, the year of the waterfront strike, and called it *All Visitors Ashore*[3] – a novel that did no harm at all to Curnow-Stead relations. In fact, Allen enjoyed and admired it.

The arguments on either side of this 'Wystan to Carlos' debate were quite complicated and Terry covers them very well. I knew Allen was not pleased, but I've only learned from the biography that he made so many pages of dissenting notes about it. As Terry records it, it was surely one of the most civil differences ever in the history of New Zealand poetry, though now and then there was an edge. When Allen mocked the practitioners of 'open form' as 'the Open Brethren' I replied that if there was an Open Brethren there was a Closed Brethren too, and I suggested that on their behalf he might be suffering from 'critical agoraphobia'.

Oddly the one suggestion in my lecture he really couldn't bear was a speculative footnote suggesting that the irregular setting of one of the new poems in *Trees, Effigies* might have been influenced by the young poets of the magazine that called itself *Freed*. This provoked his one public response – a letter to *Islands* insisting this was not so, *Freed* had 'passed unnoticed by me'. When I grumbled about this letter and said (very unreasonably) that Allen was 'sniping at me', his reply was immensely touching. 'Sniping at you was, & is, as far from my mind as from my heart, & the latter has been much troubled by feeling that so it must appear.'

Looking back, it strikes me that my position in this argument could not be either right or wrong: it was just the choice of a position – a new one, and different from Allen's – for looking at the recent history of our poetry. Sturm suggests I was displaying what Harold Bloom calls 'the anxiety of influence', 'the need of a younger poet to assert himself against the influence of a powerful poetic forebear'.

That's an entirely reasonable suggestion. And yet the evidence of Allen's sensitivities about that eight-, ten- or twelve-year gap (depending on how you count) remains; and the fact of it remains unexplained. Even in these two books the gap can't be disguised or wished away, though attempts seem to be made. We hear from Terry Sturm what we heard from Allen, that there wasn't really a gap – it's just that the poems that emerged in 1972 took a long time to write. Ten years: that is a long time – certainly not poems coming 'as the leaves to the tree'; it's scouts' pace rather than Keats's pace. In the *Collected Poems* on page one hundred and thirty-seven we have the heading 'A Small Room with Large Windows' and the date 1962 – but the poem of that title was written in 1957. We have his New York poem of 1961, and a new heading 'Poems from the 1960s', which begins with 'On the Tour', the satiric piece he wrote deploring the all-white All Black tour of South Africa in 1960. It's a poem that doesn't belong in a collection which rightly leaves out the whole of Whim Wham.[4] Why is it there then? I think to fill the gap. Then we have three poems Allen chose not to publish, two from 1961 and one from 1966 – and still, even with those questionable inclusions, you have six years to wait before the new – the really new – Curnow begins to emerge. It seems to me the harder you try to fill that gap the more obvious it becomes, the more real it feels.

It's not deplorable, not reprehensible, not in any sense a failure: it's simply a fact. When Allen was writing the *Incorrigible Music* poems and sending them to me as they were written, I questioned his 'had to' syntax in a number of them – Giuliano 'bled where he *had to* bleed', was 'dead where he *had to* die', the kahawhai '*had to* swim close to the rocks', and so on; and he was to deploy the same syntax when he came to the wonderful 'Moro Assassinato' sequence. His reply was that all the '*had to*' syntax represented 'the incorrigibleness' of existence. These things happened because they *had to* happen. I suppose my argument was for the *incorrigibleness* of literary history. There was a ten-year gap in production because there had to be; because history required it of him. It was, at the very least, kinder than the James K. Baxter fiction would have been, an idea which even now has an awful plausibility about it.

Back to Tohunga Crescent: cross-Crescent relations were good. The 1982 collection, *You will now when you get there*, went back and forth between us and, with the Raynor poem and 'Organo et Libitum', seemed to be another step forward in range. He counted on getting my reaction to every new poem, and he dedicated that book to me. I was spending more time away overseas – on leave in 1977, away a couple of months each year in 1979, 1980 and 1981, away two terms with Kay and the daughters in 1984; and in August 1986, at the age of fifty-three, I left the university altogether and flew off to teach at the Yeats Summer School in Sligo. My London contacts included Karl Miller whom I'd known since that 1977 leave when I'd taught in his Modernist course at UCL; and I'd been writing since then for his *London Review of Books*. I interested Karl in Curnow's work and he let me review the 1988 collection *Continuum*. That review in turn alerted Seamus Heaney, who was influential in seeing Curnow received the Queen's Gold Medal for Poetry.

From now on, as Sturm recounts it, it was all plain sailing. When we launched his last book in the first week of March 2001, I was able to say it was fifty years almost to the day since I'd first seen him – in enrolment week in the first week of March 1951, when I arrived at Auckland University as an eighteen-year-old student and he arrived from Christchurch as a thirty-nine-year-old lecturer. He inscribed the copy he gave me of that last book, 'For Karl, always "somewhere in earshot"' knowing I would recognise that as coming from Yeats: 'Pardon old fathers if you still remain / Somewhere in earshot for the story's end'. He must have known the story's end was close, and in fact it came in September of that year when I was in France.

Allen had been such a *presence* in my life, such an important one, during that half century – so of course I wouldn't want the biography to be other than positive and a celebration, which it is; but I do wish it gave more a feeling of the complex personal reality. Allen's character included a tendency to vanity and arrogance, in tandem with high intelligence which kept them in check. There are very occasional glimpses of these in the biography – for example the letter on page four hundred and seventy-one where he refers to the Literary Fund Advisory Committee as 'my inferiors' and says he won't have his work 'pawed and passed around among them'. Terry Sturm had chaired that committee for some years (as I did briefly), so one can imagine what he thought of that; but he makes no comment and the narrative quickly shuts down on it.[5]

If I'd said to Terry, 'You knew *that* Curnow, as we all did. Why is he not here?' Terry would probably have said, 'It's not that kind of book.' And the ghost of Jeny would have popped up with her mantra, 'We are very private people'. She always said 'We'. But Allen was also a very *public* person. He became the manager of an image, custodian of a brand. Interviews had to be vetted and approved. Poems had to be paid for at whatever his agent in Australia called 'the going rate', never mind the consequences for other contributors to a New Zealand publication. He and Jeny represented themselves as the successful literary man-and-wife, going about the world graciously receiving honours and never putting a foot wrong. The larrikin-radical was out of sight, though he was still up there somewhere among the pohutukawa, and he could take you by surprise over the dinner table.

These two books are 'a fitting tribute'. The biography is a formidable piece of research and writing – and then of editing by Linda Cassells after Terry Sturm's death – and I salute them both. It doesn't seem to me likely that you will find better readings of the poems, or a more thorough and accurate account of the making of the Curnow oeuvre over six or seven decades. But this is every inch an *official,* an *authorised,* biography; and I do think occasional glimpses of its subject from the outside, as others encountered him, with whatever reservations, would have made it all just that essential fraction more plausible, more real, more life-like.

Shortly after Allen's death, the bach on Lone Kauri Road was sold, but the name remained on the letter box with the final letter, the w, missing. This produced one of a small number of poems about Allen that have crept up on me from time to time, and I'll conclude by reading it. It's called 'Curno', spelled without the w:

CURNO

The name on the box on Lone Kauri Road
                             has a letter missing
standing perhaps for 'without' –
without the one who has gone on a very long journey.

         Under nikau and karaka in the half light
or among manuka and kauri
                      Piwaiwaka flits and taunts.
The poet was her friend but when the time came
she brought her unwelcome message.
      The stream had its say but only in opal and silver.

He was master and mentor, the hard mind,
the cool old man who wouldn't say his prayers
   or pay his dues; the long memory, the cleverest wit,
               the abominable temper, the diplomat.

       Today the beach has turned itself around,
a flat sand plain all the way out
to Paratahi Rock. The lagoon is gone.

       Sky-high improbable clouds
             float like fleeces,
and from the rocks the ghost of a poet fishes
for metaphor and cod.
            A big surf
    slams its door, and opens it,
and slams it again.

NOTES

[1] This paper was delivered on 30 October 2017 at a symposium to accompany the launch by Auckland University Press of *Simply by Sailing in a New Direction*, a biography of Allen Curnow by the late Professor Terry Sturm (edited by Linda Cassells) and of *The Collected Poems of Allen Curnow*, edited first by Sturm, and then after his death by Elizabeth Caffin. The Symposium's first panel was called 'Remembering Allen Curnow', and this was the opening paper. It is a personal response to the two books.
[2] *Pound, Yeats, Eliot and the Modernist Movement*, Macmillan (UK), Rutgers University Press (US) 1986.
[3] The Harvill Press, 1984.
[4] Whim Wham was the pseudonym over which he wrote weekly satiric poems for local newspapers. He was always quite firm that they should not be mixed with his serious poetry. 'On the tour' was a broadsheet in the Whim Wham manner.
[5] I note that these two volumes, *Biography* and *Collected Poems*, are published with grants from Creative New Zealand, and the publisher says it could not have happened otherwise. That is the nature of poetry publishing in New Zealand and Curnow's lofty scorn for government subsidies, like A. R. D. Fairburn's, was snobbish and unworthy.

From the Archive

Issue 141, September–October 2001

NORM SIBUM

From a long piece entitled 'Bird with Yellow Plumes'. Fellow contributors to this issue include Simon Armitage, Ruth Padel, Neil Astley, Gabriel Josipovici and Roger Scruton.

BIRD WITH YELLOW PLUMES

From out of the sweetness of my soul I said,
    You there in your cage,
In the sun, on the balcony,
Holding forth, you reactionary in feathers, –
You arbiter of taste, of how well the women
Carry themselves, of art's anarchic impulse,
Why always the big production?
Can't you simply whistle
Like any self-respecting bird?

You say, for heaven's sake, throw back your
   shoulders.
You say, art is ten per cent will and the rest,
   The rest is surrender. How touching. [...]

Three Poems

NICHOLAS FRIEDMAN

TO WHOM IT MAY CONCERN, PLEASE FILL OUT THE FOLLOWING QUESTIONS AND MAIL. THIS IS A SCIENTIFIC EXPERIMENT BY DENNIS KOMSA, AGE 12.

from a note dated August 16, 1963, found sealed in a Mason jar off the New Jersey Shore

The first step says to get the message lost –
though not *too* long – so its recovery
can hold significance. In this motif,
boy puts his note to sea; hope, being brief,
dies out soon after curiosity...
And yet the jar turns up, its glass embossed

with cursive letters somehow still intact
since bobbing off in 1963.
Inside, a roughly folded questionnaire
asks little more than *how* and *when* and *where*
it steered into another's custody –
in other words, the overwhelming fact

of being. The greeting toys with fate, if not
tautology: 'TO WHOM IT MAY CONCERN...'
Scribbled in blue – half lower case, half caps –
the letter is a lesson in *perhaps*.
A tarnished nickel meant for the return
rattles the glass like a persistent thought.

A virtue, sure – but what will come to rile
our days? What if the good life means
steeling ourselves against the ordinary,
then sussing risks out like an actuary?
Even here, the common intervenes:
In fifty years, the jar sailed half a mile.

The boy, too, never left that stretch of sea,
and so his note returned like an immense
memory never made. Now, fixed in age,
he lingers near the bottom of the page,
where one last question begs uncommon sense:
Is there anything else which might help me?

Distraction Display

Some birds, to fend
against predators,
will fake a battered
or broken wing
to redirect
attention from
their young. If this
is evolution's
best guess, well,
it's not a bad one.
Just yesterday,
I saw a grackle
dragging a wing
like out-of-water
tackle, then rise
from a tuft of clover,
tracking with ripe
chokecherry eyes
as it flew up
and over me.
It lit in a maple
by a nest I'd failed,
at first, to notice –
a minor thing
to thank distraction
for, when it
came into focus.

Glass Animals

for Rory Waterman

'Not bad', you say, then nod to hide the fact
we've wasted half the afternoon by stopping.
We could be getting drunk at Chapter House,
and anyway you're right: the case is dusty,
the little cards are barely legible,
and all the jellyfish have snapped or cracked.
There's still some life left in the octopus!
It fans out like a mottled carriage dress.
'Yeah, that one's good', although two tentacles
have dropped like ballast from its palm-sized mass.
A slack rain starts to grease the windowpanes.
The ill-lit hall grows dim. The cases glow.
We hurry into jackets, tuck our chins,
and slant through slanting rain, with you ahead –
a visitor, but leading as you go.

Five Poems

MARK VALENTINE

Torn

The brook emerged
at the bend of the road
then vanished in thorns.
Where did it go? We thrust
through, wanting to know.

We didn't get very far:
it was hot, we got wet,
tore our shirts,
bare arms and legs, yet
stayed excited, for

we might find our selves
in some place we did not know,
unseen and left alone,
some rippling, hidden
secret territory, our own.

Seed

Even on those days
when the fountains
rise from marble
and flags and awnings
flap, still the black
seed is in the wind,
the dark is winged.

Kindling

The house smells of woodsmoke,
though the fires are long dead.
Who was it who lived here
watching the flames and who
tended the blaze and who
cleaned out the grate in the morning?

All one and the same, the idler
by the fire, and the emptier of
the ashes, and the brusher of
the hearth-stone – that boy with
the grey-eyed stare, who
with his pale deft fingers made
the brittle kindling live
its brief and golden time.

Cartouche

Published of sparrows
the prophecies hiss
the mysterious head
is white at meeting.
The Sleepwalker captures spirits
at Cross Dun, place of the yew.
The rowan whispers morning
the black grebe opens
the Book of Gates.
Something not snowfall
waits in the green ruins.

Ever

Peter Blackwood works on the railway
Pauses at Sleaford twice a day
And twice a day he sees inside
The rooms at number twenty-five

Next door to the tobacconist.
And thinks that surely this must
Be, if anything at all, a shop of dust
For all there ever is, is emptiness.

What Translation Can Teach

EDWIN MORGAN

A Translator's Notebook (7)
edited by James McGonigal

TRANSLATION IS AN EDUCATION. Part of its enlightening effect comes from opening a door onto the context of the original poem and the cultural influences on its author. Another part comes from its effect on the translator's own writing. This section of Translator's Notebook takes Morgan's engagement with Hispanic poetry further, beginning with a poet known to Federico García Lorca. It then looks back to Morgan's translation of sixteenth- and nineteenth-century Spanish poetry, with just a glance towards his future engagement with Brazilian Portuguese. Morgan's letters reveal how long-standing the influence of translating could be, as he recalls and shares what he has learned. Since he was a generous teacher as well as a poet, such advice was educational too. It was not information merely, but knowledge carried 'by heart', sometimes across decades until released by an enquiry.

In September 1991, Sam Gilliland, a young Scottish poet working on a collection, *After Lorca*, had sent poems for comment. Morgan mentioned his own enthusiasm for Lorca, and also for Luis Cernuda who, shocked by Lorca's assassination, went into exile in several countries including Scotland, working briefly at Glasgow University. In the 1950s, Morgan had translated his 'Cementerio de la ciudad' as 'A Glasgow Cemetery'. Gilliland was also a translator, interested in Mário de Sá-Carneiro, who committed suicide in Paris in 1916 aged twenty-six, while planning with Fernando Pessoa a third issue of *Orpheu*, a short-lived journal of Portuguese modernism:

> 13 September 1991
> Dear Sam
> You are quite right about Cernuda and his Glasgow poem. I am enclosing a version of it I had in my *Rites of Passage* book, for your interest. It certainly suggests he found the city a fairly grim northern place after Seville, though the poem is wonderfully atmospheric. The translation was included in a play about Cernuda which was put on by Strathclyde [University] students in 1988 and which I saw; the play suggested that although unhappy in Glasgow he was not devoid of solace (like Lorca he was homosexual). I did not meet him at Glasgow University – he arrived not long before I was called up and he had gone when I came back after the end of the war. I was much interested by your account of Sá-Carneiro, and it would be very good if you could manage to bring out a collection of translations, as he is simply not known here but by all accounts ought to be – especially as Pessoa's name has gradually made its way, through translations, in recent years. [...]

Born in Seville in 1902, Cernuda moved to Madrid and became a member of the 'Generation of 27', the group of poets and artists that included Lorca, Pedro Salinas, Rafael Alberti, Dámaso Alonso and Vicente Aleixandre. In *Los Placeres Prohibidos* (1931), Cernuda used surrealism to explore his homosexuality, and his work was influential in Spain in its directness of approach to his gay identity. After Lorca was murdered in 1936, Cernuda fled to England, working as a teacher in Cranleigh before moving to Glasgow University to teach Spanish, from where he travelled to the east and then west coast of the United States and finally to Mexico City. Morgan never met him, but probably knew by the 1950s of his fleeting presence in Glasgow. 'Cementerio de la ciudad' appears in J. M. Cohen's *Penguin Book of Spanish Verse*, first published in 1956, and the holograph text of 'A Glasgow Cemetery' dates his translation to 23 December of that same year. It was published in *The Voice of Scotland* VIII: 3 & 4 in Spring 1958 and in *Collected Translations* (CT): 268.

Morgan's letter to Gilliland describes the poem as 'wonderfully atmospheric'. It is worth looking at the 'atmospherics' of the final two stanzas of the poem to discover the translator's response to Cernuda's reaction to his city. (Cohen's prose version precedes the Spanish and English):

> When the shadows fall from the crowded sky and the smoke of the factories settles as grey dust, voices come from the pub, and then a passing train shakes its long echoes like a wrathful trumpet.
>
> It is not the judgement yet, oh nameless dead. Be calm and sleep; sleep if you can. Perhaps God also is forgetting you.

Cuando la sombra cae desde el cielo nublado
Y el humo de las fábricas se aquieta
En polvo gris, vienen de la taverna voces,
Y luego un tren que pasa
Agita largos ecos como un bronce iracundo.

No es el juicio aun, muertos anónimos.
Sosegáos, dormir; dormir si es que podéis.
Acaso Dios también se olvida de vosotros.

Dusk comes down out of a cloudy sky;
smoke from the factories floats off, lost
soon in grey dust; voices are heard from the pub;
then one passing train
shudders and echoes loud like a black trumpet blast.

Not the last judgement yet: sleep, if you can,
Sleep on, anonymous dead, in your long calm.
God too perhaps forgets you, not just man.

There is a sense of the city's greater activity (even from the peaceful vantage point of a graveyard) in Morgan's version. The use of independent clauses in the first stanza quoted clearly helps, divided by semi-colons into a series if sense-impressions or snapshots. And each element seems active – dusk 'comes down' instead of falling; smoke 'floats off' instead of settling; the voices are not simply coming from the pub but being overheard by the poet who is registering the scene. This contrasts with the dependent followed by an independent clause in Cernuda's poem, where the focus is on the reflective mind of the observer as much as on the activities of the scene itself – 'when this happens, then that happens, and then the train that passes makes this sound [...]'. Morgan's passing train has two verbs rather than one, and its particularised 'trumpet' ends with a real black blast, marking the stroke of Doomsday. (There may be a nod here to Scottish reformer John Knox's *First Blast of the Trumpet Against the Monstrous Regiment of Women* (1558); his statue stands in the Necropolis behind Glasgow Cathedral.) In any case, this more dynamic sense of energy suggests Morgan's ease with industrial Glasgow and his deep sense of belonging there, as compared with the displaced Spanish observer, belonging neither with living nor dead.

In the last stanza of Morgan's version, there is a skilful deferral of the phrase 'anonymous dead', almost drawing out the eternity of death. This is partly also to gain an equivalence to the half-rhyme and alliteration of the original, using 'can / calm / man' for sound effects, although the monosyllables of English also contribute to an atmosphere of quiet certainty about death and the graveyard, alongside the uncertain memory of God. This is skilful. Yet perhaps, despite Morgan's preference for accuracy in translation (as against Ezra Pound's or Robert Lowell's variations on the source text) we are being presented with a slightly different version of the poem. Cernuda's unease is being redressed in favour of the city of his exile.

*

Angél Flores, an American editor and academic, had approached Morgan to translate Petrarchan poets for his current project, *An Anthology of Spanish Poetry from Garcilaso to García Lorca* (Doubleday, 1961). He replied by offering Flores some versions of Lorca, Cernuda and Neruda in January 1959, and said he would be glad to do more of Neruda 'whom I find very attractive'. In the event, copyright expenses for Neruda's work were prohibitive. Flores was willing to see all these moderns, although his main intention seemed to be to interest Morgan in Garcilaso de la Vega and 'the almost totally unknown Rosalía de Castro', the nineteenth-century Galician poet.

Flores had originally contacted him in October 1958 on the recommendation of Hugh MacDiarmid, who admired Morgan's translation of Heine into Scots in the *Saltire Review* (III:9, Winter 1956). Flores, who taught Modern Languages in Queens College, New York, was then editing *An Anthology of German Poetry from Hölderlin to Rilke in English Translation* (Doubleday, 1960). Morgan sent him seven translations of August Graf von Platen (1796–1835). He was so impressed that he thought Morgan must be teaching in the German Department of Glasgow University, and wrote to him there. Morgan also translated Joseph von Eichendorf, Heinrich Heine (the latter in Scots) and a further five sonnets from Platen for this German anthology.

These German poems are not as distant as we might think from the Spanish translations. Writing to Flores in October 1958, Morgan made specific reference to Platen's 'very curious "Gaselen"' with their repeated rhymes. These are in the form of ghazels (or ghazals), the Arabic/Persian love poems of loss or longing that are found in divans or poetry collections. The Platen translations thus look back towards Lorca's Andalusian gacelas in *Diván Del Tamarit* (1936), and forward to Morgan's own *The New Divan* (1977). His first translations of Platen were 'Forfairn's My Hert' ('forfairn' means forlorn, abused) and 'Time and Space, Torment', gloomily dated 13 November 1949 and 29 January 1950 respectively. Morgan's later 'Introduction to Platen' in CT: 308 hints at similarities between poet and translator. Both had followed war service with university study:

> His career was punctuated by more or less unhappy homosexual affairs, which are often dealt with in his poetry in a surprisingly lightly coded way. He was a master of many poetic forms, including adaptations of classical and oriental metres, and his work has the permanent interest of that kind of writing where tight technical control fails to conceal a depth of romantic feeling.

That was written in 1996. Earlier, Morgan doubtless felt constrained to employ more circumspect coding. His Platen translations did not appear in *Rites of Passage* (1976), but in a limited edition of one hundred and fifty numbered copies from Castlelaw Press in the Scottish Borders, *Platen: Selected Poems* (1978). Here is a short example of the Gaselen in this collection:

> Whitely the lily wavers in the waters, to and fro:
> Yet you can never say, my friend, 'It falters, to and fro.'
> Its foot is rooted there so fast in the deep sea bed
> Its head just cradles love, rocks love thoughts to and fro.
> ('Im Wasser wogt die Lilie...' CT: 313)

A sense of identification with the foreign poet was often a key factor in Edwin Morgan's approach to translation. But how far back can such identification reach, and how can it relate to cultural forms, such as Renaissance poetry, that seem radically different from modern life and art? This question relates to the Petrarchan poetry that Morgan was now called upon to translate. When he resumed civilian life and academic study in Glasgow after the War, Morgan began a series of notebooks which he called *GNotelibriks* 1–4. Here he kept track of his reading and thinking by quotation and translation from a range of authors. We find many Renaissance sonnets copied out in French, from Ronsard, Du Bellay and Maurice Scève. Scève seems particularly significant in terms of self-identification, especially in his use of anonymity and veiled authorship, with poems being signed by initials only or by enigmatic mottos or emblems – creating a hidden personality that must have seemed attuned to Morgan's self-protective anonymity at this time.

In particular, he was drawn to Scève's ten-line decasyllabic 'dizains', which he found 'reminiscent of a sonnet in general effect', but seeming 'to pack more meaning into less bulk through involuted syntax'. These poems also seemed to enact a state of mind where the lover 'is dissolved, like his purely physical longings, into an abyss of nescience, a gulf of oblivion' (Introduction to Morgan's

Fifty Renascence Love Poems, 1975; and CT: 161). He also admires the way that Scève manages to bring his widely varying moods into the traditional Petrarchan structures, and so renew and extend these. For a gay person in search of 'an impossible perfect partner' (as Morgan once recalled Quentin Crisp describing his own quest) the Petrarchan convention of unattainable distance between poet and beloved must also have retained a particular resonance into the post-war decades. Certainly his personal life at this time enacted such a sense of distance.

In his talk to the Literary Society in Bristol University in December 1956 (see 'Translator's Notebook 3', *PNR* 235) Morgan had commented on the surprising number of lyrics in the standard anthologies of English poetry that are in fact translations:

> Wyatt and Surrey, Drummond and Campion, Herrick and Cowley – a large number of their poems are translated from French, Italian, Latin or Greek. Sometimes among their best or best-known work – Surrey's sonnet 'Set me whereas the sun doth parch the green', or Wyatt's 'My galley charged with forgetfulness' (both from Petrarch).

And he wonders who actually wrote these poems that were Italian but have become English.

Now at the beginning of January 1960 he turned to Spanish near-contemporaries of those poets: to Fray Luis de León (1527–91) with 'Vida retirada', 'Oda a Francisco Salinas' and 'Noche Serena', as well as Garcilaso de la Vega's 'Egloga Primera' (ll. 239–47) and 'Nemeroso' (all of these being in the Cohen anthology). Flores would publish six of Morgan's translations of Garcilaso, and the three of Fray Luis mentioned. The uncollected translations are really too long to print, and Morgan's view of them is deftly summarised in the 'Introduction' to *Fifty Renascence Love Poems* (1975), reprinted in CT: 159–63, where his admiration for Garcilaso rings clear. The collection was published by Whiteknights Press, linked to the University of Reading where Ian Fletcher of the English Department had an editorial role. This press had also published Morgan's *Poems from Eugenio Montale* (1959), while he was in the process of translating these Spanish devotional and Petrarchan poems.

Since Fray Luis de León does not survive into any of Morgan's collected works, it might be fair to look at how even in the most dutiful of translations (and Flores was a determined and deadline-driven editor) Morgan's skill is evident. Apart from historical and cultural differences of Renaissance verse, he had to deal with the relative ease of finding rhymes in Spanish as compared with English. We find him using assonance and alliteration to create an equivalence, together with a careful use of connotation and rhythm to keep his own versions lively. For example, here is the fourth stanza of Fray Luis de León's 'Vida Retirada':

> What pleasures can it bring me to be pointed at by vain fingers, or run in pursuit of that wind [of fame] breathless with sharp longings and mortal cares?
>
> [J. M. Cohen, *Penguin Book of Spanish Verse*: 151]

Qué presta a mi contento
si soy del vano dedo señalado?

si en busca de este viento
ando desalentado
con ansias vivas, con mortal cuidado?

Why should my heart be glad
If thoughtless fingers point out where I go?
If I lose what breath I have
Seeking the windy goal
Where desperate cares and burning longings roam?

Here, I like 'thoughtless fingers' for the 'vain fingers' of the prose translation or 'the vain finger' of the original, being more idiomatic – as also is the opening question with its three key monosyllabic beats, emphasizing Morgan's use of the physical connotations of 'heart' instead of the more generalized 'pleasures' or 'happiness'. The assonance or para-rhyme works well (as in 'glad'/'have' or 'go'/'goal') as does the expressive use of iambic pentameter to clinch that final line. So although Fray Luis did not make it into *Fifty Renascence Love Poems* because of his religious themes, we can admire the professionalism that Morgan brought to the task, and understand why Flores kept pressing him for more.

*

Despite his normal university workload, Morgan responded quite quickly and dutifully to these promptings, although he often found it impossible to focus on creative work during term time. Translations and original poetry both had to be postponed until the vacations. But I think he was impressed by the Spanish-American editor's can-do energy (as he would later be by Michael Schmidt's approach at Carcanet Press) and he worked on Flores's suggestions. His version of Manrique's 'Coplas por la muerte de su padre' appeared in Flores's *An Anthology of Medieval Lyrics* (1961, New York: Random House), and 'Romance del Conde Arnaldos' in his *Medieval Age* (1964, New York, Dell Publishing).

But he warmed most obviously to his editor's enthusiasm for Rosalía de Castro (1837–85), who wrote in her native Galician as well as Castilian. Morgan devoted a concentrated period to her poetry in early August 1959, and on the 20th he sent Flores twelve poems (CT: 383–89). Five of these were published in *Spanish Poetry from Garcilaso to García Lorca*. All are from her final collection, *En las orillas del Sar* (1884) (*On the Banks of the River Sar*), mainly written while she was suffering from terminal cancer.

Morgan may have been drawn to her partly because earlier she had chosen to write in Galician, unused as a literary language for many centuries. In the 1950s, of course, he himself had been exploring the use of Scots as a medium of translation, notably for Heine, Platen, Mayakovsky and Shakespeare. Its use in poetry involved a political dimension, combining a sense of nationalism with socialist solidarity towards working-class culture and speech. Rosalía de Castro reveals in some of her work a passionate sense of social justice, as in her 'Justicio de los hombres!, yo te busco' or 'Cuando sopla el Norte duro' (CT: 385, 383–4), and this theme is clearly represented in Morgan's selection from her collection.

There were also attractive cultural links between Scotland and Galicia, its name being derived from the Roman

Calaica, Land of the Celts. Her earlier collection *Cantares gallegos* (*Galician Songs*) (1863) had a considerable impact there and beyond (her husband Manuel Martínez Murguía was a noted editor, regionalist promoter and archivist). Based on popular motifs and singable cadences, the collection is framed by poems by 'the lively bagpipe girl' ('*la meniña gaitera*'). Morgan's literary interest in Scots language was largely in tune with Hugh MacDiarmid's ground-breaking use of an eclectic or 'plastic' Scots (as it was called in the 1950s), taking words and expressions from different historical periods, dialects and linguistic registers to force forward a new medium of rebirth on a former nation that had come to view its own history in a defeatist or sentimentalised way. (Morgan favoured the inclusion of urban speech, however, compared with MacDiarmid's rural emphasis.) So this linguistic or 'cultural nationalist' aspect of Rosalía de Castro's work would have been important to Morgan. Her work had also been championed by Lorca and Cernuda.

Another attraction for him might have been the way her poetry was marked by Northern '*suadede*', a combination of nostalgia, longing and melancholy that doubtless appealed to Morgan during a period of sadness and disconnection in his personal life. Here is a comparison of prose and poetic translation on that melancholy note, again using Cohen's anthology (324–5):

I do not know what I am eternally seeking on earth, in the air, and in the sky: I do not know what I am seeking, but it is something that I lost I know not when, and that I do not find even when I dream that it invisibly pervades all that I touch and all that I see. Happiness, I shall never find you again on earth, in the air, or in the sky, even though I know that you exist and are not an empty dream.

Ya no sé lo que busca eternamente
en la tierra, en el aire y en el cielo;
yo no sé lo que busco; pero es algo
que perdí no sé cuando y que no encuentro,
aun cuandoe que invisible habita
en todo cuanto toco y cuanto veo.

Felicidad, no he de volver a hallarte
en la tierra, en el aire, ni en el cielo,
　aun cuando sé que existes
　y no eres vano sueño.

I do not even know what it is I am searching for
Through earth and air and sky without rest;
I do not know what my search is for, but
It is for something I lost – I do not know when –
And never find again, though I dream it lives
Unseen in everything I see and sense.

O happiness, shall I never surprise you in hiding
Once more, in sky or air or on earth,
　Even though I know you exist,
　No dream, no idle guess!
　　(CT: 388)

The word '*saudade*' for loss and deep longing reminds us of the links between Galician and Portuguese, two anciently-related languages separated off by politics and cultural change, rather as Scots and English were. If he read Rosalía de Castro's Galician poems, these might have been Morgan's first introduction to the linguistic culture of the Noigandres group. In Brazil, there is a national Saudade Day on 30 January, but Morgan's experience of translating the Brazilian concrete poets was of joyful engagement with like-minded comrades in the avant-garde. Those will be discussed in the next section of 'Translator's Notebook'.

Yet there must have been an uplift too in his discovery of Rosalía de Castro. Something was learned by heart, to judge from this excerpt from a letter to Michael Schmidt, composed almost sixteen years after Morgan had translated her. He and Schmidt were working on permissions for *Rites of Passage*, so this situation may have brought the Ángel Flores anthology to mind. Three of Schmidt's poems had just been translated for Octavio Paz's *Plural*:

7 February 1975

Dear Caballero

[...] I have had no reply yet from Cape regarding Enzenberger's poem 'Konjunctur' – I wrote on 10 January. Have they by any chance been in touch with you? If not, I had better give them a reminder. I believe that Suhrkamp's British agent Rosica Colin in London is to be in touch with you direct about the Enzenberger poems; I wrote to Suhrkamp on 9 January and they replied on 21 January saying they had passed my letter to Rosica Colin, asking her to contact you.

Congratulations on being put into Spanish. Do you ever write in Spanish or translate your own poems into it? My mind is full of such thoughts as I have just returned from the University of Warwick where I was lecturing on 'Nationalism in Poetry'. [...]

Coming up by train today from Birmingham to Glasgow was absolutely celestial – blue sky all the way, crisscrossed by vapour-trails from jets that seemed to be playing like whales, and all the time that hot extraordinary February sun – I had Virginia Woolf on my lap but instead I wrote a poem (poem and a half actually) – it was impossible not to be glued to the window – 'Dicen que no hablan las plantas, ni las fuentes, ni los pájaros...' but it's not true it's not true!

That final quotation is from Rosalía de Castro: 'They say that plants can't talk, nor springs of water, nor the birds [...]'. This is a well known poem in *En las Orillas del Sar*, although not one that Morgan had tackled. It did appear in the Spanish anthology, but translated by Kate Flores, wife of the editor. But he had clearly read it. Its persistence in the memory is sweet and extraordinary. And what of the poem and a half written on that journey? Well, the Glasgow University library's list of his holograph poems records poem eighty-one of 'The New Divan' as being composed on the date of that journey. It begins, and continues, lyrically:

The night is over, the lark is singing,
the sages sit in full divan
in the anteroom of heaven,
the water bubbles, the pipe is sweet.

This poem, however, is immediately answered by the bitter saudade of poem eighty-two (dated 7/8 February), the longest and one of the most affecting of the whole Divan. It reminds us what learning by heart must also entail:

> We never knew we'd have no more
> to feel except one pain, one glow
> memory blows us to, like coal.
> (*Collected Poems*: 322–3)

At this complex conjunction of poetry and prose, railway lines and jet trails, Spain and Arabia, tenderness and pain, actuality and memory, it seems apt that, for Morgan, translation enters to play its unifying, educative role.

Five Poems

LEO BOIX

Cycles

'We love the things we love for what they are.'
Robert Frost

Blackbird's gone
        – until next year's
           bonanza. He left
a simple cup nest full
of dried twigs, hairs
        – courtyard detritus
barely hanging on
a wisteria climber
that never flowers
        its badly grafted roots
compressed, down
into our house's under
        – side. It's been here
since we moved in
30 July 2009.
        – It grew faster, taller
           than we first thought.
Love witness, even these
thunderous wrens
        – *Troglodytes* like to catch
hidden flies, tiny spiders
dangling over light-green
        – leaves, shoots. These signs
        we've learned to read
every English summer
        – almost by chance.

Syllabic Tales

I

Now he watches birds until implosion, crystals falling,
        sparks of unknown words
goldfinches
        call –
a liquid song

II

To the River Plate to see water hyacinths in flower,
        hearts of sun-scorched mud –
once he was
        there
at Quilmes quay

III

For the millionth time returning to his land, to bury
        his dead forebears –
come here, look
        down
at your own past

Peregrination

I crossed the bridge
        there was nothing

one cup
      of cold coffee
one coin from Argentina
an eyeball on a plate
my mother singing *Me olvidé de vivir*

I turn back
      gather my things.

The Somnambulist

    counts backwards
    as if there was a language just for chairs.
    Sluggish. From evening until noon
    witch hazel he has not planted
    wait for that unknown light.
    Oblique moth equilibrium,
    iridescence. A timed
    retreat to the garden
    and wait.

    And wait,
    retreat to the garden,
    iridescence. A timed
    oblique moth equilibrium,
    wait for that unknown light.
    Witch hazel he has not planted.
    Sluggish from evening until noon
    as if there was a language just for chairs,
    count backwards.

Motifs

I – Truncated creatures

Your parents left because of a knock –
Somebody inside? – at their door.

Luggage, two kids, an English dictionary,
things for a new life. You thought of darker days.

II – Objects on head

Equilibrium, childhood birds
balancing on your bushy eyebrows.

La soga que gira y gira, la soga gira que te gira
You played with sister's dolls, your only companions.

III – Backsides, their emissions

When you kissed Iván in the attic
Mother heard you downstairs. A sign:

Be quiet, boy. She sensed
a tower burning.

IV – Readers

A poem by Borges turned your old patio
into a summer's day. Incantation.

A game of chess – you against sun, lapwings, toads.
Grandmother feeding demons in the garden.

V – Inside receptacles

Your house turned into an egg,
it broke when she died.

You moved, once again
to a hollow tree for owls.

Heightened from Life

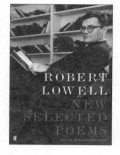

Robert Lowell, *New Selected Poems* (Faber) £14.99

Reviewed by RUTH HAWTHORN

At the San Francisco Poets on Poetry conference in 1979, Susan Gilbert recalls a panel on 'contemporaries' where one speaker stood up to proclaim, 'Catullus is my contemporary and Pound is my contemporary, and Whitman is my contemporary, and Bly is my contemporary, but Robert Lowell is *not* my contemporary'. This rather pompous declaration was met with 'applause, laughter, and some cheers', a response that, as Gilbert points out, was indicative of the general turn against Lowell which was in motion by the end of the 1970s. Lowell, with his ambivalent politics, his well-publicised breakdowns and his controversial inclusion of personal letters in the volume *The Dolphin* (1973), became a distinctly unfashionable figure. His stock had fallen dramatically, and by the late 1970s there were few who still held him to be 'the greatest American poet of the mid-century', as he had so often been lauded during his lifetime.

Following the 2003 edition of Lowell's *Collected Poems*, there was a resurgence of interest in his work but the reviewers remained divided on his merits and, often, his most vehement defenders did as much to obscure his complex achievement as his detractors. Commentators who reified Lowell as 'The Voice of America', as 'the major American poet of his generation', as 'prophetic' set him up as being authoritarian, monumental and transparent, propounding the division between him and those avant-garde poets who have been oppositionally championed as wary of direct statement and deliberately evasive of a coherent lyric subject. This is, of course, an unhelpful dichotomy as so much of Lowell's poetry is uncertain, uncomfortable and self-cancelling. Even his signature lists of adjectives are frequently diminishing ('Cured, I am frizzled, stale and small'), distorting ('a snapshot, / lurid, rapid, garish, grouped, / heightened from life') or indicative of limitations ('Poor measured, neurotic man').

It is this less grandiose side of Lowell which Katie Peterson foregrounds in her centenary edition, *New Selected Poems*: 'The Robert Lowell I offer in this brief selection emphasizes the perishability of life, its twinned quality of fragility and repetition, as framed by the structured evanescence of daily consciousness', and she champions him as a poet who has been 'wrecking the monument all along'. Peterson's introduction is novel and ambitious, only briefly touching on the well-worn ground of *The Dolphin* debate and avoiding lurid biographical details which have so often overshadowed attention to the poetry. While she aims to offer a rounded coverage of 'the events of the life' through her selections, she leaves the task of telling the life to the poems themselves and also dedicates space to 'poems memorable for their language, not simply the vanishing facts of story'.

Peterson acknowledges a difficulty in curating Lowell's work for a twenty-first-century audience; the issue of identity politics, which was central to the decline in his popularity from the late 1970s, is now even more acute:

> In a certain political neighbourhood of our contemporary world we like to use the word 'privilege' to describe people such as Lowell – white, male, funded, educated, carriers of social position and family name (two of his cousins were notable American poets, and his mother was descended from a Constitution signer). Lately, in American poetry, we like not liking people like that, and we distrust privilege as we would a mask.

Some of Peterson's attempts to recuperate Lowell's image and advance the case that he is a poet we should still be reading are more successful than others. Her links to Facebook and 'the information explosion of the Internet' feel a little forced and her reading of 'Skunk Hour' as an example of Lowell 'checking his privilege', even with the inverted commas, overreaches. It may be true that 'birth is an accident' but Peterson's contention when reading 'Sailing Home from Rapallo' that 'death fades family names and disintegrates the hallmarks of prestige' is less convincing. The poem exists to witness the error and reflect on the irony that 'In the grandiloquent lettering on Mother's coffin / Lowell had been misspelled LOVEL'. As Elizabeth Bishop commented, with some frustration, Lowell's family history meant all he had to do was to 'put down the names' for a poem to seem 'significant, illustrative, American'. Some of Lowell's more overtly political poems are explicitly concerned with the hierarchies and politics of commemoration. 'For the Union Dead' centres around 'St Gauden's shaking Civil War relief' which 'sticks like a fishbone / in the city's throat'. It is a poem where Lowell very publically uses his position of cultural prestige to comment on Boston's racial inequalities, but it also repeats (however ambivalently) the individualised valorisation of Colonel Shaw against the backdrop of 'his bell-cheeked Negro infantry'. Shaw's heroism is accented through his commitment to die with 'his black soldiers', who remain an undifferentiated mass throughout the poem.

However, none of this means we shouldn't read Lowell (or that in reading Lowell, we are somehow precluded from reading widely among other poets whose perspective isn't coloured by privilege). Indeed, these are generative and fascinating tensions in his work which are reflected in Peterson's edition. She has decisively managed the immense task of narrowing down Lowell's sprawling oeuvre. Her selections are compelling, offering a balanced overview of his career. From the forbidding New England of *Lord Weary's Castle* (1947), through anthology favourites like 'Skunk Hour' and onto lesserknown lyrics from his final collection *Day by Day* (1977), Lowell is here in all his perplexing variety.

Cadenzas for Typewriter

Jonathan Blunk, *James Wright: A Life in Poetry* (Farrar, Straus & Giroux) £29.50

Reviewed by TONY ROBERTS

James Wright found in poetry a disciplined means of self-preservation against the mental torment and alcohol-fuelled mayhem his life sought. A fine poet and charismatic teacher grounded in the metrical tradition and New Criticism, he followed a different path to the so-called Confessional, the Beat and the New York poets of the period, prompted by his assimilation of Latin verse and the poetry of Germany and South America. In *The Branch Will Not Break* (1963) and *Shall We Gather at the River* (1968), probably his best known collections, he moved toward freer forms which could accommodate the vernacular and eventually prose.

Wright, the man, lived at a pitch of intensity which sends the reader reeling. His selected letters, *A Wild Perfection*, reveal a passionate and restlessly experimental figure. He can be 'hysterical and profane', humiliated and deeply apologetic, compassionate and brutally frank. He knew his gift, if at times faint-heartedly, but was also his own most merciless critic. Of his first collection, *The Green Wall* (1957), he wrote it 'stank'; his second, *Saint Judas* (1959), was '*still* second rate' and he was to describe *Two Citizens* (1973) in an appreciative letter to Dave Smith, the poet who had reviewed it with 'intelligent good will', as a 'botched effort', a 'bad book'. The letters give a visceral sense both of Wright's demanding expectations of his work and what it cost him in his search for technique.

His mental states were fuelled by a bipolar condition that wreaked havoc with the life and the poetry at times. In May 1958 he wrote to his teacher John Crowe Ransom: 'If I could curb my personal hysterias, then perhaps by the same token I could purge my verses of their violence.' In the following year he told James Dickey, 'I have been getting the shuddering horrors, indescribably so, and frequently going to pieces, sometimes in really mad and violent ways [...] Worst of it is that it hits me as pure egoism.' Two years later he confessed to Anne Sexton, 'in my real self, I am way off in the darkness, and sometimes the light, dazzled beyond vanity, at war with sloth'. Industry caused the pressures it kept at bay. In the mid-1970s he was still able to write of attacks in which he felt 'a loneliness of the soul, in which I feel an appalling sense of abandonment and loss'. Such turbulence alternated with periods of calm, with amazing productivity and with generosity and genuine feeling for family, friends and students.

Wright grew up unhappily in the town of Martin's Ferry, Ohio, on the West Virginia border ('that unspeakable rat-hole'), where his father worked for the Hazel-Atlas Glass factory. It gave Wright a subject: the desperation of lives, the dark waters of the Ohio River and of the self. As Robert Hass explained, his famous preoccupation with 'the suffering of other people, particularly the lost and the derelict, is actually a part of his own emotional life. It is what he writes from, not what he writes about'.

After a year's absence from school caused by a nervous breakdown, Wright began 'to rise from the dead'. Recognising that the GI Bill would fund his studies, he enlisted in the post-war army at graduation, which took him to Japan. In 1948 he enrolled at Kenyon College in Gambier, Ohio, where he learnt German, began translating poets and contributed to Ransom's *Kenyon Review*. Graduating with honours, he married and received a Fulbright Scholarship to study German literature in Vienna. There he discovered Trakl's poetry. The following year Wright enrolled in graduate school at the University of Washington in Seattle, with the intention of preparing for settled employment teaching literature.

Those years, 1954–56, were crucial in his development. He was taught by Theodore Roethke and Stanley Kunitz, met Richard Hugo, Carolyn Kizer and David Wagoner. He also began a life-long correspondence with Donald Hall. While working on his PhD (on Dickens), his first collection, *The Green Wall*, was chosen by Auden for the Yale Series of Young Poets. In 1957 Wright began teaching at the University of Minnesota. He struck up friendships with James Dickey and Robert Bly, with whom he visited and worked on translations.

In 1959 Wright's depression and heavy drinking contributed to his separation from his wife and children. It was also the year in which his second collection, *Saint Judas*, was published and in which he immersed himself in Spanish and Latin American poetry. He continued to co-publish translations of Trakl and Vallejo, extended friendships (Louis Simpson, John Logan) and was denied tenure at Minnesota:

> At that time I was so god damned miserable that the only thing I could do was translate Theodor Storm from German, have a bad love affair, get sick, go to hospital, get visited by John Berryman (who went and taught my class while I was sick), get habitually drunk, teach very well when I could bring myself to make a class, and, naturally, get fired.

He then taught at Macalester College in Saint Paul. *The Branch Will Not Break* was published to acclaim, especially for its 'deep image' poetry (with its surrealism and sentimentality). In 1966 he began teaching at Hunter College, at which time he met his second wife and the couple began their love affair with Europe. He published *Shall We Gather at the River* as well as translating poems by Neruda, before being awarded the Pulitzer Prize for his *Collected Poems* (1971). *Two Citizens* appeared two years later. There were periods of exhilarating European travel and depression brought on by stress, but the awards, appointments and poetry continued to come: *Moments of the Italian Sumer* (1976); *To a Blossoming Pear Tree* (1977); and posthumously *This Journey* (1982). Wright attended a White House tribute to American poets in 1980, the year in which he died of cancer at fifty-three. Five years before his death he had acknowledged: 'I have inflicted a good deal of pain on others and on myself during my lifetime. But God know I have suffered inwardly quite enough hell to pay for it.'

It is Jonathan Blunk's job to deal with that. His authorised biography follows slowly on the heels of *Above the River: The Complete Poems of James Wright* (1990) and the 2005 *Selected Letters* (to which he made a significant contribution). It is a sympathetic yet judicious biography and a necessary corrective to the self-laceration in Wright's letters. It also conveys the immense vitality of the man for whom poetry, as Donald Hall wrote, was life. The particular danger with a rollercoaster life like Wright's is for his biographer to be distracted by the drunken antics and lose touch with the work. Blunk avoids that. He gives insight into the unpublished journals as well and, while encouraging his reader to look to the collections for the poems, still manages to explore a good number of them.

That Blunk knows his subject is made clear at the outset, where he focuses on the critical summer of 1958 when, with one collection behind him and a second effectively completed, Wright seriously debated quitting poetry. We are then shown the prolific adolescent composer of sonnets and apprised frequently of the hundreds of poem drafts Wright produced even before publishing. He had, as his biographer explains, a 'musical intellect'. A 'typewriter is for me simply a piano on which to improvise melodies and fragments' he wrote. He could not stop.

Wright was also possessed of a phenomenal memory that allowed him to recite comprehensively in public which, along with a sonorous voice, contributed to his popularity.

Blunk is abetted throughout the biography by the deployment of shrewd insights and assessments from Wright's friends and those blisteringly revealing comments of the man himself. For example, to his semi-fictional muse, Jenny, he wrote in 1959 of his total dedication: 'It is the struggle between my inner self (poetry, for which I apologised in order to *live*) and the horrible gray world of deterministic hopelessness where I was born and which I only partly escaped.' And in the last decade of his life, joying in southern Europe, he confessed, 'I'm getting sort of tired of the darkness. There is something to be said for the light, also, after all.' In his work he had moved beyond compassion to what one critic called 'benevolence and grace'.

Wright once said he wanted 'to be a grown man'. His sense of un-entitlement confounded this for years. Blunk's fine biography illustrates that the trajectory of his life, like that of his work, was towards a maturing, more uncluttered identification with the light. Reading this biography – with *Above the River* and *A Wild Perfection* to hand – is an inspiring experience.

The Lyrical Task

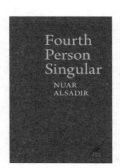

Nuar Alsadir, *Fourth Person Singular* (Liverpool University Press) £9.99; Leontia Flynn, *The Radio* (Cape) £9.99

Reviewed by SASHA DUGDALE

Nuar Alsadir's *Fourth Person Singular* is a subtle and occupying book. I've been carrying it round for months in my tote bag and in my head, returning to it in libraries, on trains, discovering notes I made on the text, forgetting a detail then and rereading it in a sort of déjà-vu – wondering if I had had that thought myself, if it had welled out of my own unconscious, or if it had been planted there by Alsadir at an earlier reading. It's the seismograph of a never-still brain. Perhaps ironically, for all the insistence on the conditional nature of consciousness in Alsadir's texts, I was heartened every time I read it by the sure knowledge that there was a consciousness like mine (like yours), constantly turning over, a car engine at the lights, generating endless associative and lyrical threads of thoughts. Like all literature worth its salt, it recalls the familiar neural engine in new ways.

Fourth Person Singular opens with a series of fragmentary lyrical thoughts, many of which are resplendent in their truthfulness about thought and consciousness:

> Thinking off the page: a plane circling over its destination, waiting for a signal to land.

> A text message in the night poked into my dreams like a magnetic rod and scrambled them, redistributing the metal shavings.

These 'shavings' laid out associatively, a constant quick-witted interior monologue with no exterior motivation, reminded me of the brilliant asides in a nineteenth-century novel, but all put together, without the endless social detail, the suicides, the mud, the arduous journeys. It's a way of writing, fragmentary, distilled, claiming for itself the unmediated interior lyrical thought without its usual formal decoration, that seems particularly current, perhaps practised more in the US, but about to hit the UK like a tidal wave – looking aslant at the grand narratives, as it does. It has the advantage of pressing at the problem (of creativity/authenticity) with a kind of honesty the lyric doesn't have, disowning the lyric, whilst simultaneously stealing all its furniture.

However, Nuar Alsadir's particular originality in the genre lies in the way she explores the lyric self from the point of view of both psychoanalyst and poet, breaking down and intermingling the two disciplines. In a recent article for *Granta*, Alsadir describes a clowning workshop she attended, in which the participants were encouraged to break open 'their prototypes' and 'create paths towards the unsocialised self'. Here, a parallel writing exercise presents a series of short pieces she writes at night and without preparation when the alarm clock rings at three fifteen a.m. This sudden wakening will supposedly allow her to write with immediacy, to access Mina Loy's 'sublime core', perhaps to surprise it into revealing its position. It's a playful section, the immediacy emphasised by the inclusion of an image of her scrawly night-writing, and yet the whole venture coloured by knowing failure, since however spontaneous the texts might have been, displayed in a book like this and bracketed with a description, they become the prototypes they seek to elude.

The heart of the book is a mini-essay, which uses both physics and psychoanalysis to describe the relationship between the lyric ego and its addressee. The essay develops the idea that both utterance and personae have multiple time and space reverberations and a dynamic 'circuit of communication' defines the lyric utterance, just as it defines all other social relationships. The resulting term for the lyrical ego becomes 'fourth person singular' – a conjugation allowing the necessary multitudes, and perhaps a happy escape for lyric from the shame of lonely confession and self-indulgence.

*

Leontia Flynn's *The Radio* tackles the lyrical task head on, and with no qualms about the authorial persona. In fact, the collection gives the reader a virtuosic and almost flamboyant formal performance: odes, sonnets, tributes to writers who have gone before, the knowing borrowing of a poet who knows her originality is held in a balance with heritage. It's a book which very palpably comes of age, performing the rejection of unconscious, unformed youth and anxiety of influence, nowhere more clearly than in a fine tightly rhymed elegy to Seamus Heaney, 'August 30th 2013', which responds to Heaney's 'Elegy' for Lowell. Flynn considers Heaney's lines about Lowell: 'The way we're living, timorous or bold, will have been our life', and owns up to timorousness, drifting, writing in an idiom Heaney might essentially have disapproved of for being 'written with intention' and 'unfiltered', whilst questioning the usefulness of continuing to write like Heaney in a new world.

But how to get beyond the shame of being younger, a woman, and born to a somehow lesser age? Or how to write as a 'messed up woman poet with Daddy issues', as the poet asks on behalf of a generation. One implicit suggestion is through technique, Flynn's own elegy showing a very fine ease with the form, twisting it to her own idiom, and making rhymes from the detritus that make up this inescapable 'centrally-heated', 'crowd-sourced' world. But the poem ends with a deliberately lyrical and Heaney-esque imperative: 'Now shut up. Write / for joy. Be deliberate and unafraid.'

The collection has two title poems. In the first and longest 'The Radio', Flynn tackles the legacy of the Troubles through the lens of the childrearing years of her mother, 'small, freaked out, pragmatic, vigilant'. The family move out of Belfast to the country and the horror and violence reach them only through the radio's drip of news, their mother standing sentinel to guard them from the worst, to keep them alive:

> So daily the radio drops its explosive news
> and daily my mother turns to field the blow.
> The words fall down, a little neutral now,
> onto the stone-cold, cold, stone kitchen floor.

It's a wonderful, poignant, bitter poem. The slow pace of the longer poem, here and elsewhere, gives Flynn so many opportunities for enlarging, adding novelistic poignant detail, excelling at the domestic space. Here she reflects on motherhood, the 'centripetal force' of growing children, and the 'Heart of Darkness' that is motherhood in war against a backdrop of birdsong, cows, Valium and concrete walls. Placed alongside is a concrete poem 'Listening to My Mother Listen to the Radio': a box made of the busy words 'The Word The World' and a terrifying empty space in the centre of the box with the two words 'The World' in it. The poem will have numerous interpretations, but for me that bare space was the fearful listening mind, unable to banish thoughts of the outside world, even amidst the constant noise of words.

Flynn's voice is wry, grim on occasion, conversational, wide-ranging, technical. It's a deliberate collection and it follows its own imperative: unafraid of its voice, and joyful in a gritty way, laying out the costs and causes of joy simultaneously.

Heart's Granary

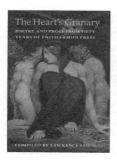

Lawrence Sail (ed.), *The Heart's Granary: Poetry and Prose from Fifty Years of Enitharmon Press* (Enitharmon) £30

Reviewed by ALISON BRACKENBURY

When I think, admiringly, of Enitharmon Press, I recall one book, in particular, Phoebe Hesketh's *Netting the Sun*. The title is a fine definition of poetry. The front cover displays a bold drawing of black willow against a gold sun – well fitted to Hesketh's clear, tough poems. The back cover features a tribute by A. Alvarez to this 'absurdly underrated' poet. I now realise that, in 1989, when I bought this cherished book, Enitharmon Press was already twenty-two years old.

The Heart's Granary is colourfully punctuated by Enitharmon covers and illustrations, including a delectable trio by Hockney. Besides poetry, Enitharmon's publications include artists' books, limited editions and original prints. Lawrence Sail, the heroic harvester of this anthology, notes that Enitharmon 'has had only two directors: Alan Clodd, for the first twenty years […] Stephen Stuart-Smith for the next thirty'.

How did Sail select from fifty years of poetry and prose? He explains, disarmingly, that he chose 'what most appeals to me and seems to succeed best on its own ground'. He also aimed to show Enitharmon's range. Poetry and prose are kept separate, ordered by theme. All writers and artists are impeccably indexed.

Sail shows a light editorial touch. Through almost four hundred pages, readers are revived by living links between his selections. 'There will be blackbirds' promises U. A. Fanthorpe, published by Enitharmon, after Peterloo Poets closed. 'So have I heard bird-song, beneath the / trajectory zone, at Passchendaele,' writes David Jones. This birdsong comes from *Wedding Poems*, published in 1930, republished by Enitharmon in 2002, a lifetime later.

Many of my highlights from this anthology come from poets who may have been, in some way, 'absurdly underrated'. Yet they have a loyal readership, well-served, even created, by Enitharmon. They include poets who bring deep freshness to traditional form. Phoebe Hesketh turns lullaby to lament in 'I Give Death to a Son':

> Trailing glory and slime
> he is washed and dried,
> grave-clothes ready warmed
> by the fireside.

Ruth Pitter is another poet I know and value, thanks to Enitharmon. *The Heart's Granary* stores her piercingly simple lines about swifts: 'So they go over, so they go by […] high and high and high in the diamond light'. A different clarity marks Isaac Rosenberg's 'August 1914' (which includes the phrase: 'The heart's dear granary'). Rosenberg, eloquent sardonic outsider, may still remain outside listings of great poets from his Great War: 'Droll rat, they would shoot you if they knew / Your cosmopolitan sympathies'. From the Movement, should the sensitive, technically superb work of Elizabeth Jennings also be more widely known? Here are her tender lines to 'my father and my mother': 'And time itself's a feather / Touching them gently'.

This anthology frequently celebrates late flowering. Jenny Joseph was often overshadowed by her much-anthologised 'Warning'. But her last Enitharmon collection, *Nothing But Love,* features recklessly good love poems: 'O cherry, O open heart'. In Seamus Heaney's rendering of Robert Henryson's medieval masterpiece, *The Testament of Cresseid*, the ageing speaker watches a winter planet, 'lovely Venus, beauty of the night':

> I thought to pray her high magnificence,
> But hindered by that freezing arctic air
> Returned into my chamber to the fire

I hope some readers may add Henryson to their winter granary. First, in this anthology, they may travel the world, including Spain, with Lorca, and Somalia, where Maxamed Xaashi Dhamac 'Gaarriye' offers his striking insights into poetry: 'It's riding bareback on an unbroken horse' (translated by W. N. Herbert and Martin Orwin). Finally, readers may explore bracing landscapes of new poets, including Nancy Campbell's 'Arctic snowstorm'. Blizzards of quotation would fail to represent Sail's prose choices. They include 'Milking', a grim tale by Edward Thomas, relieved by 'cold apple dumplings with cheese, and cowslip wine'. As Christopher Middleton wisely writes in his 'Epilogue': 'Poetic understandings are […] narrow unless grounded'.

On the front cover of *The Heart's Granary*, Blake's black-draped Enitharmon sits huddled on the ground. Lawrence Sail's history of Enitharmon Press concludes: 'Arts Council England funding came to an end in March 2017'. Due to this, and to adverse changes in bookselling and the wider economy, *The Heart's Granary* is the last new title from Enitharmon Press. But all is not dark. The firm has merged with Enitharmon Editions, which continues to publish artists' books. All of the Enitharmon Press backlist remains in print, actively promoted and, when necessary, reprinted. So if you discover new appealing authors in this anthology, you can still buy their Enitharmon collections. I recommend Enitharmon's own website, which offers Phoebe Hesketh's *Netting the Sun* for half the price currently quoted by one online bookseller.

What is offered by *The Heart's Granary*? In general, poetry characterised by beauty and eloquence, free of pretension. In particular, the voices of poets valiantly championed by Enitharmon, such as Frances Cornford, in 'Epitaph for Everyman': 'O passer-by, my heart was like your own'.

Life Writing

Kumukanda by Kayo Chingonyi (Chatto & Windus) £9.99; *Night Sky with Exit Wounds* by Ocean Vuong (Cape) £9.99

Reviewed by PHOEBE POWER

This review brings together two debut collections, each by an author who grew up far from his birthplace: Kayo Chingonyi was born in Zambia, Ocean Vuong in Vietnam; the poets write from London and New York respectively. Broadly speaking, these books are about coming of age, taking into account layers of memories, family histories and political events which all contribute to self-understanding. This surface comparison, however, belies the distinct character of each of these collections, in particular their form and style. Vuong's work is serious and painstaking, unpredictable and in places beautiful; Chingonyi's is lighter and more relaxed, energised by the precision of specific details.

The first section of *Kumukanda*, with poems fuelled by a nostalgic passion for nineties radio music, is for me its most vital part. 'Self-Portrait as a Garage Emcee' is a dense, five-page tour-de-force of interwoven memories. There is a disorientating sense of place, as the speaker begins at 'Harold Hill, Essex', before being reminded of the high-rise view from his previous, south London home: 'the River Wandle a coiled snake', and the tiny intimate details of that community, 'where Sacha blasts / a tattered ball into the goal-net simulacrum'. The proper nouns here, chosen for their sparkling particularity, pattern a playful diction that is at once affectionate and surprising. Chingonyi's long form allows the poem to explore the unsettled space between his old home and the new one in Essex, until the discovery of 'Majik FM' and the music he loves becomes the speaker's route to security. The narrative shift which then takes place is a key achievement of the poem, when while raiding his 'mum's cache of cassettes', the speaker comes across 'a black TDK, unmarked', containing the recorded voice of his father with the 'twang of a lost tongue'. This moment is like a fissure in the poem, something that looks outside of the conscious construction of the self as 'Emcee' and allows a different category of emotion, another voice and a different self, to edge into the picture. It is Chingonyi's capacity to open out form in multiple directions, gathering memories in unexpected ways, which makes this poem compelling.

The other long sequence in the collection, 'calling a spade a spade' also accumulates meaning in a way that can be more rewarding than in shorter works. The ten deft poems in this section, each of eleven lines, gather a series of memories about being black and treated differently; this ranges from being cast with 'the only other *other* / kid in class' as the Magi in the school nativity ('Alterity'), to the pressure to practise 'self-effacement' at drama school ('The Conservatoire System'), to being limited to the parts of 'lean dark men who may have guns' ('Casting'). Like Claudia Rankine's *Citizen* (2014), the sequence reveals the insidious sedimentation, within a consciousness, of the effects of years of casual racism. By tracing the development of an acting career, Chingonyi's text asks a further question: how much freedom do we have to construct our own identities and roles? In particular, Chingonyi addresses the equivocal status of 'The N Word', which might be reappropriated by a black voice, 'making wine from the bad blood of history', and yet does not lose its power to hurt, 'knocking me about the head'.

The violent potential of affective language also resonates strongly in Ocean Vuong's collection. Language is literally embodied: for example, the letter *d* is a 'strand of black hair – unraveled / from the alphabet' ('The Gift'), a smile is 'a white hyphen where his lips should be' ('Immigrant Haibun'); and hands have 'syllables / inside them' ('A Little Closer to the Edge'). The conflation of body and language has a relationship to the wounds and bullet holes which also recur, as where 'words / entered me' ('Logophobia'), or when looking through the 'entry wound' made by a gun, the speaker might 'see the end of this / sentence' ('Always & Forever'). This imagery is extraordinary and encourages the reader to engage with Vuong's own syllables and words as an affective, at times painful, and even mystical experience. Vuong's command of image can be tremendous:

> Let every river envy
> our mouths. Let every kiss hit the body
>
> like a season. Where apples thunder
> the earth with red hooves. & I am your son.
>   ('A Little Closer to the Edge')

Metaphor is masterfully employed here to express the sensuality of emotion; 'red' is typical of Vuong's sensitivity to colour elsewhere in the book, as is the animal physicality indicated by 'hooves'. Sometimes titles can also play a large part as emotional signifiers, especially those with mythical references. 'Telemachus' is a gorgeous poem of discovery, the son turning over his shipwrecked father to look into the 'cathedral / in his sea-black eyes'. The longing for Odysseus's homecoming felt by his son is appropriated by the contemporary speaker in the service of his own depth of feeling for his absent father, and renewed through the use of Vuong's own metaphor. This emotional depth is layered further with the freight of recent conflict, 'the bombed / cathedral' adding a modern shade to the density of this powerful complex of hurt and love. The burning city in 'Trojan' similarly mythologises the 1975 fall of Saigon, the subject of the following poem 'Aubade with Burning City', while 'Immigrant Haibun' describes an Odyssey, or Aeneid-like abandonment of this city in the context of modern migration.

The multiple layerings of myth, family relationships and recent global history create a powerful opening section to the collection. As the poems progress, forms continue to shift, with spacing and line-breaks employed in myriad ways to suggest different kinds of pause and rhythmic energy; for example, 'On Earth We're Briefly Gorgeous' moves from three-line stanzas to fragments spaced across the page, to single-line sentences and prose blocks; other poems shift lines from one side of the page to the other, as if turning the head, continuously stretching and changing perspective:

> I am swinging open
>   the passenger door. I am running
> toward a rusted horizon, running
>
> out of a country
>
> to run out of.
>   ('In Newport I Watch My Father Lay his Cheek to a Beached Dolphin's Wet Back')

These continual variations on end-stopping and enjambment create an organic progression, charting an unpredictable but ever-moving course through the collection. Nevertheless, the tempo and tone remain largely the same – tense and slow – making the book as a whole a solemn journey for the reader. At times, I found myself wishing for a little levity within the spiritual search, or a greater indication of the external world in the more self-reflective poems. In comparison, Chingonyi's book looks outwards to society, at its best grounded in a London realism 'where alleys wake to condom wrappers' ('Andrews Corner') which is part of what must be noticed and expressed. For Vuong, such details have a different status, where an image such as 'newports torn condoms' is the necessary backdrop to a poem's climax of self-understanding, focused on the subject's guilt surrounding casual sex: 'you haven't learnt the purpose of *forgive me*' ('Because It's Summer'). Chingonyi's scene is generous and non-judgemental; Vuong's is a site of anxiety. *Kumukanda* is a rapid and vitalising read, while the slow release of tension in *Night Sky with Exit Wounds* might be best experienced in a quiet garden, aloud, one spell-like poem at a time.

CARCANET

award-winning and shortlisted poetry collections

SINÉAD MORRISSEY *On Balance*

winner of the Forward Prize for Poetry (Best Collection)
shortlisted for the Costa Book Awards

CAROLINE BIRD *In These Days of Prohibition*
ROBERT MINHINNICK *Diary of the Last Man*
TARA BERGIN *The Tragic Death of Eleanor Marx*

shortlisted for the T.S. Eliot Prize

available at carcanet.co.uk and in all good book shops

Currencies

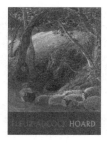

Fleur Adcock, *Hoard* (Bloodaxe)
£9.95

Reviewed by SUE LEIGH

The cover of Fleur Adcock's latest book (Samuel Palmer's burgeoning golden apple tree) and its title evoke richness, plenty. As the back cover blurb explains, these are poems that have been hoarded away for some years and have now been brought to light. The title also recalls the Anglo-Saxon kenning *wordhord* – that storehouse of language that is the poet's stock-in-trade.

'Loot', the first of the fifty poems (which are arranged in four sections) revisits a personal coin collection. Of a Coventry halfpenny the poet writes, 'I used to see it in the hand of Pepys' and imagines it jingling in a pocket with a farthing, a silver groat. The slow accumulation of coins might not be that dissimilar to the gathering of poems – 'one delicious coin after another, / in [...] unheard of currencies'. Other poems in this section relate to the writer's art, including 'Six Typewriters' and the delightful 'Her Usual Hand': 'If handwriting mirrors character / all I can see mine reflecting is / my headlong scramble for the exit, / shouting something over my shoulder.'

These three poems are typical of many in their conversational ease and autobiographical content. Adcock is fascinated by the past and her ancestors. In 'Mother's Knee' she recalls family stories about children – 'no dates, no writing'. With the benefit of hindsight, she reveals a darker fate for one child but offers: 'You surely can't like that knowing that? Better / to leave her in 1880-something / prancing in Slippery Creek in her shift'. In her darkly strange poem 'A Game of 500' she writes, 'The Muse is a seeker after sensation. / She wants me to tell you.'

There are poems about her schooldays ('Mnemonic' recalls a rhyme for remembering the genders of third declension Latin nouns – 'Nothing I write will be as durable'), life as an impoverished student in London and her work as a librarian. Adcock is open about her personal life, her politics. A brief unsuccessful second marriage and tender feelings for the child of her first are brought together in the moving and disturbing 'The Sleeping-bag'.

Two sequences of poems about Ellen Wilkinson (who led the Jarrow March in 1936) bring the Labour politician vividly to life through anecdote, small detail: an apple-green dress against her shingled red hair, how small she was 'taking three steps to every man', the stray dog that joined the march, her 'pop star exit'. Adcock is interested in the minutiae of a life: 'I want all the notes and scribbles you burned, the private diaries you never kept [...] I want your voice.' But this intimate close up is precisely what she gives us.

Adcock considers old age, the physical changes that accompany it and mortality but always with a sense of lightness. 'Real Estate' reveals a determined independence, a zest for life as she responds to a neighbour's suggestion that she downsizes. 'A little flat! / One with no room for half my books, no stairs / to keep my knees in flexible order, / one in which on no morning would my eyes / open to next door's silver birch, self-sown.'

Adcock is alert to the contemporary world. In 'Hortus' she dreams a walk 'through cliff-top gardens enamelled / in greens' and finds her fingers 'fidget / for a mouse to click on Save and store it / among my Favourites, to revisit'. Although she is not always enamoured of this world. The loss of bookshops for example and of computers she writes, 'I shall say nothing'.

There are bursts of lyricism in several poems about plants and animals. In the short sequence 'A Spinney' the loss of a crab apple and elm are weighed against the planting of a yew seedling, a conker: 'A green hand shoots up, / [...] a fistful of sticky buds for next spring.' Two dogs are the focus of the hugely enjoyable 'Oscar and Henry'. Environmental concern is expressed in 'Albatross', her homage to Coleridge. '*It ate the food it ne'er had eat*'. Albatross now feed their chicks on plastic debris from the ocean.

The poems in the last section describe Adcock's visit to the North Island of New Zealand in 2015 – a kind of road trip – and reflect the mixed feelings she has for the country of her birth. These are poems about remembering, change. As she says in 'Miramar Revisited', she is 'puzzling out directions [...] Reason doesn't seem to prevail on a sense / lodged as deep as my pituitary gland. / But we're not lost. We've made our expedition.'

Our Accents Mix

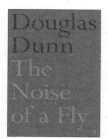

Douglas Dunn, *The Noise of a Fly* (Faber) £10.99

Reviewed by RORY WATERMAN

It's been seventeen years since Douglas Dunn's last collection. The first poem here, 'Idleness', implies it might not have been so long, perhaps with intimations of chaos theory for what is to come:

> Can you hear them? The flap of a butterfly.
> The unfolding wing of a resting wren.
> The sigh of an exhausted garden-ghost.
> A poem trapped in an empty fountain pen.

There is a lot of what might have been in this book, and of what once was: 'the scent of one who is no longer here', or the fact that 'Something about ageing makes me witness youth / Surviving in me like a troublesome / Dilemma'. This is coupled with a clear imperative, which has perhaps always been Dunn's greatest strength, to 'face what happens without self-pity', as he writes in 'Fragility', and to try to say things as they are, or were. As he self-cautions in '*Wondrous Strange*', another tentative *ars poetica*, 'I must ask / My Muse to save me from contriving / A forger's touch of moonlight on the page'.

Dunn's tongue is often close to his cheek in even the book's most sombre poems of *memento mori*. In 'The Wash', in which he writes, 'I don't feel like Sisyphus, I feel like his boulder', the ageing poet asks: 'How long does a book, or sheet of paper, last? / If the answer is hundreds of years, does that console? / Go early to bed and outstare the clock'. Dunn retired about midway between his last collection and this. The poems 'Thursday' and 'Leaving the Office', next to one another here, make a pair, the former a funny-not-funny take on feeling 'boring' while still lecturing and 'putting extra pennies' towards retirement, and the second a pensive, unsentimental description of being 'oh-so-very-gently shoved / Towards the book-loaded van and a pension'.

It does get a bit monotonous at times, though, and this really shows through in the weaker pieces. A poem beginning 'Posh totty totter past on serious heels', but which is really a tired poem about being old ('I too was young'), isn't saved by bearing an epigraph from Shakespeare's 'Sonnet I'. The versification can be jaw-droppingly slack in places, too, considering this poet's often startling gift for putting the right words in the right order. The doggerelly rhyming in 'Recipes and Refugees' doesn't exactly lend the poem much gravitas:

> Affluence in exotic recipes –
> The choice of what to cook is international.
> I welcome that, but think of refugees
> Drawing their water from a flyblown well
> In the lands of falafel and couscous
> Where sympathy is worse than useless.

In addition to being the author of some exceptionally beautiful and emotionally complex lyric poems, Dunn has also often tended towards the prosaic, and many of the poems here are not exceptions. In 'The House of the Blind', we are told that Louis Braille 'accidentally put his eye out / With an awl in his father's workshop', and that 'Thomas Edison invented the gramophone / To provide speaking books for the blind' (he was also a horrible bastard and if you don't believe me look him up), before the non-epiphany that 'I write / To be read by eyes, and mind, and fingers'.

The two often converging leitmotifs of this collection, then, are ageing and writing poems. If there is a third, it is flora, often acting as a mute counterpoint to incessant deterioration, like Yeats's wild swans: 'spring's predictable daffodils / Bulging yellow silences, snowdrops and crocus / Already gone', as 'The Wash' has it. Or it is a cheery accompaniment to a memory, as in 'Provence': 'And there was me, and there was you / In the fair grass-tide'. Towards the end of the book there are also several longer poems about places – a confusing Italian town, a villa on Lake Balaton in Hungary – though they don't generally go far beyond the diary or the guidebook. But the collection's longest and penultimate poem, the meandering 'English (A Scottish Essay)', comprising one unbroken run of about two hundred and fifty lines of loose pentameters, is also one of the finest pieces here, in part for its polemical forthrightness:

> In our new parliament, our accents mix
> With confidence – get that into our lyrics!
> No one's branded by a vocal stigma,
> By mystical public schools or Oxbridge,
> By England's creepy, sad, vocal enigma,
> That patronising sound of patronage.

There is certainly plenty of fire and passion left in this poet.

A Thousand Words

Sinéad Morrissey, *On Balance*
(Carcanet) £9.99

Reviewed by ADAM HEARDMAN

At an event last year in Newcastle, Sinead Morrissey introduced her poem, 'Millihelen', by defining its title-word: a unit measuring the amount of beauty required to launch a single ship, rather than the mythical 1K. Helen over a thousand. A 'fanciful' idea, a note on the text tells us, but with a deliberate borrowing from the modes of utility. The poems in Morrissey's sixth volume enact, variously, this idea of constituent parts versus wholes, empirical observation by the light of things less tangible. At what point, if ever, Morrissey appears to ask, does something become more than the sum of its parts? The poems achieve a sort of magic, but also show their working-out in the margins – reading them feels like taking apart a clock while it still ticks, or holding a still-beating heart. In 'Millihelen', set at the launching of the *Titanic* in Belfast, we occupy a:

> moment swollen with catgut-
> about-to-snap with ice picks hawks' wings
> pine needles eggshells

The fluid syntax also somehow isolates each word, each line, exposing the 'units' of language even as it quickens their flow. We feel each rivet and bolt of the creaking ship as it gulps out into the impossible sea 'as though it were ordinary'.

As though anything were ordinary, Morrissey celebrates the often-blurry boundary between the mundane and the miraculous. 'Mayfly', a stunning poem dedicated to pioneering aviator Lilian Bland, tricks about in the accidental awkwardnesses of the English language – in phrases like 'Conspicuously mischristened' and 'may-fly // may-not fly' the poem is picked apart as though by a child fascinated with clockwork, like Bland's aircraft built with 'improbable Victorian pram wheels'; 'a whiskey bottle'; 'an ear trumpet'. From this hacking assembly, the plane and the poem achieve impossible lift-off:

> the tracks
> of her passage in the spangled grass,
> and then their absence –
>
> your footprint missing on earth for the span
> of a furlong, as if a giant had lifted its boot
> and then set it down.

And once we're unmoored in this beyond, the trick is to find a new balance. Morrissey's poetry, and poetry in general, wobbling between fact and fiction and eventually settling somewhere else, often achieves it. '[I]n fact everything regains its equilibrium.'

Not every poem in the collection pulls it off. 'My Life According to You' and 'My Seventeenth Century Girlhood' play the same games with perspective and voice that were done to greater effect in poems like '1801' and 'Blog' in Morrissey's blockbuster collection *Parallax*. But at its brilliant best, *On Balance* is the work of a true engineer-artist, like the thirteenth-century Ismail al-Jazari (who provides the cover-image and the inspiration for the final poem) who believed, according to Morrissey, 'all visible things // the über-florid signature of God'.

'At the Balancing Lakes' measures tragedy against objective detail with a child's detached, egalitarian perspective – which could be either cold naivety or profound and intuitive understanding:

> A girl is drowning.
>   A cuckoo is throwing
> Its voice in the trees

And if looking at the world through this lens is a kind of warped experience, it's also a return to perspectival origins in order to rebuild. We are, as in the al-Jazari poem, like:

>   dismantled
> humanoid automata
> reconstructing themselves
>
> from the bottom
> up

In one poem, to get our 'singing ticket to the afterlife', to gain admittance, we must 'post ourselves into it, limb by limb'. In another, 'the dead are legion, / eager to speak & awaiting / a Wireless Telegraph / System to usher them in'. Morrissey's poems are folksy, but they're also a wireless technology, a conduit for those things – the dead, the marginalised, the voicelessly infant – who are eager to speak, but lack the nuts and bolts of expression. Like al-Jazari's drawings, these poems are problem-solvers, their moments of beauty and soul seeming latent to their emotional utility. They're doing the same work as those captivating sketches, but, on balance, maybe a thousand words say more than a picture.

Going, Going

Cain, Luke Kennard (Penned in the Margins) £9.99

Reviewed by ROWLAND BAGNALL

> – *I really gotta go. You don' make sense.*
> – *I don't try to. Get with it.*
> John Berryman, The Dream Songs (1964–68)

I recently went to hear Luke Kennard give a reading in the sunlight-filled conservatory of the Botanical Gardens in Oxford. It was uncomfortably hot and the humid air was difficult to breathe. Towards the end of the event, as Kennard read from his latest collection, *Cain* (2016), I felt as though I'd drifted into something else entirely, my clothes now sticking to my skin. This was no longer the experience I'd signed up for, but something more, like I was being gently punished for a crime I didn't commit but which I'd somehow been seduced into confessing I was guilty of.

Cain is a book concerned with making sense: of Cain, of art, of us, of it. 'That you were *marked* all scholars can agree', begins the opening poem, which examines the various religious and imaginative understandings of the Old Testament Cain, 'but where, how, why and if it worked presents / the reader some perplexity'. *Cain* is full of marks and their interpretations, from the man whose family has arranged to have him exorcised – although the priest finds nothing wrong with him – to a culture unaccountably obsessed with zombies.

The central interrogation of the book presents a fictionalised Luke Kennard, who, after suffering the irreversible loss of 'my faith and my marriage in the same week,' is visited by Cain in the (dis-)guise of a Community Psychiatric Nurse. With Cain's guidance, Kennard tries to find an answer to the question, What does *me* mean?, looking back into his childhood, an attempt to understand his self.

It's a coincidence that I read Max Porter's *Grief is the Thing with Feathers* (2015) almost immediately after *Cain*, in which a recently widowed Dad is dropped in on by Ted Hughes's multipurpose Crow – '*I won't leave until you don't need me any more*' – appealing for a comparison I don't have space to stitch out here. This being said, it's Berryman that flickers at the edges of this book, whose Henry skates among *The Dream Songs*' many voices, pains, and secrecies, as if he were a long-lost relative of Cain's. 'Our breakdowns guarantee us', assures 'Dream Song 226', just like the scars and imperfections that we hope ensure our life's distinct.

'Berryman was best! / He wrote like wet paper maché', sings Nick Cave on his 2008 album, *Dig, Lazarus, Dig!!!*, which I think applies to Kennard, too. The central section of *Cain* is a sequence of thirty-one anagrams, shaped and re-shaped from the paper maché letters of Genesis 4, verses 9–12, where Cain resides. The anagrams are sculpted into the surreal narrative of a fictional televisions show – starring the eponymous Cain, Kennard (now 'Father K'), and their mutual love interest, Adah – surrounded in red text by their own imagined commentary.

Although Kennard draws our attention to Gregory Bett's collection *If Language* (2005), the anagrams direct us to a labyrinth of references, luring us into the complex labour of decoding them, like David Foster Wallace's project of balancing work and fun, pleasure and discomfort for the readers of *Infinite Jest* (1996). It's a coincidence, also, that 2017 saw the return of David Lynch and Mark Frost's televisions series *Twin Peaks* (1990–91), which arguably inaugurated the culture of devotional television-watching that exists today. Indeed, this sense of religiosity and the pressures of exegesis are affirmed by the anagrams' visual resemblance to an ancient scriptural text, while the commentaries themselves appear to signal to the prose sections of *La Vita Nuova* (c.1295), in which Dante offers meanings for the thirty-one poems he brings together, matching Kennard's number of anagrams.

Cain is a difficult book, but difficult books can be good for us. Like the television show at its centre, it combines form with experiment, terror with comfort, and punishment with reward. Above all, however, Kennard surveys the gulf between how we are perceived by others and how we see ourselves, 'embroidering excuses / on excuses, weaving our own safety-nets'. It is a remarkable achievement, it is for now, and it is not to be fought. 'That's like trying / to steer out of the skid,' says Cain: 'intuitive, understandable / but completely unhelpful. You steer *into* / the skid, you regain control. Perverse, but...'

On the Irwell's Sunny Shore

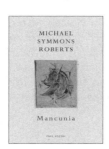

Michael Symmons Roberts,
Mancunia (Cape) £10

Reviewed by HILARY DAVIES

What is utopia? Where is utopia? Where, and what, is Eutopia, and what is the relationship between the two? The answers proffered these days are more surprising than you might expect. But the problematic begins with the originator of the word, Thomas More, who was well aware of the pun on these two pseudo-Greek neologisms, no-place and good-place. Is the good-place unrealisable on this earth, and so a no-place? Should we even be thinking of its possibility? Any too hasty interpretation of what More either intended to praise or criticise in the society he lived in, or some putative improvement on it, has to take account of the 'frame' in which he set his dialogues: as he gently leads his friend, Raphael, to table, he muses to himself that much of what his companion has said is 'absurd' and that he 'cannot perfectly agree to everything he has related'. But these remarks, too, are hedged about with caveats and qualifications: 'However, there are many things in the commonwealth of utopia that I rather wish, than hope, to see followed in our governments'. Some of the things Raphael has just deplored are an over-estimation of the worth and the power of money, and the exploitation of the poor by the rich for their own advancement. Raphael's diatribe would not sound out of place from the mouth of that nineteenth-century explorer of the dark side of Mancunia, Friedrich Engels.

Michael Symmons Robert's latest collection of the same name is described in the flyleaf of its cover as a journey through 'an imagined city, a fallen Utopia'. Yet that is what all cities are: places where the imaginations and histories of their citizens interact and create new landscapes – dystopian, to a greater or lesser degree, in their realities. Symmons Roberts knows and sets out to explore this; in the opening poem, he 'shakes out his coat' which mysteriously seems to grow larger and larger until it is 'twice the size. / I had no sense that it was so bunched and hemmed'. Suddenly, in the next poem, he shows us where we are, approaching Mancunia/Manchester as in a plane at night, 'like embers from above [...] / now stadiums with unblinking eyes, / car lots set out as piano keys'. The city is both Lilliputian and Brobdingnagian, those other fallen utopias.

The prose riff 'A Mancunian Diorama' is a stream of consciousness that makes the Protean nature of the real/unreal city explicit. We hurtle headlong through Manchester's history, from its inception as a Roman fort on the sandstone bluff overlooking the Irwell whose name goes deeper back to the Celtic Mamucium, 'breast'; through Marx and Engels; the invention of graphene; the Peterloo massacres; the 1996 Arndale bombing of the city centre. But there are also novelists, entertainers, early virtual realities in the form of prototype computers. Symmons Robert's visions can easily sit side by side with the Republik of Mancunia, a Man United blog but also Internet micronation, begging the question about the boundaries between electronic and topographical reality.

Symmons Roberts's language is for the most part spare, his stanzas short and often in loosely rhyming couplets. This creates an impression of light-footedness, as if, like those who have preceded him in the city, his print is fading and difficult to discern: 'Raise a glass you lonely souls, / to the master of lighting small details'. But there are many subtle echoes of those earlier creators of utopias, if one knows how to look: 'The Value of Nothing' clearly alludes to Raphael's critique of money-worshippers, 'My hunch is that their true fault lay/in thinking they could change their destiny // with amethysts as amulets, deep Russian, / dark as plum-blood, worth a fortune'. As the collection builds, there are also suggestions of other types of utopia in the titles, some of which are severely ironic, but suggestive nonetheless, 'In Paradisum', 'Manichaean', 'Terra Incognita, 'Terra Nullius'. Symmons Roberts has written about the genesis of the final poem, 'Manumission' in *The Tablet,* and here we find a different acknowledgment perhaps: that utopias are not to be sought, or found, in postulation or theory, but in the messy possibilities for redemption offered by the world in which we live, 'an awakening in skin so real it hurts, / a stretch and flex and flinch under a sun that burns / [...] we / tread the streets to trace the ones we love / and find them all, remade but recognisable'.

Fish, Flesh & Fowl

Adam O'Riordan, *A Herring Famine* (Chatto & Windus) £9.99; Matthew Olzmann, *Contradictions in the Design* (Alice James Books) £12.50; Miriam Nash, *All the Prayers in the House* (Bloodaxe) £9.99

Reviewed by JOEY CONNOLLY

Adam O'Riordan's *A Herring Famine* is a book which has squarely inherited a tone and poise from the Heaney-Mahon-Donaghy-Paterson axis, with the same easy and sometimes beguiling movement between the sensual and the sweeping ostentations of history and religion. He works in the medium of the gently expressive lyric, the tone understated but no-bullshit and wise.

The problem for O'Riordan, though, is that tone in itself isn't enough for actual wisdom; it's only enough for the impression of wisdom; it beguiles but it doesn't deliver. It seems very often in *A Herring Famine* that a studied poise – the ghost of good poetry twenty-years past – is allowed to take the place of any actual search for insight. When the narrator of one poem is in Berghain, the hypercool Berlin nightclub world-famous for its techno and dark rooms for public sex, he immediately thinks 'of Dante's circles of hell, / of the room a floor below where lust was explicated endlessly' and of 'the rituals of disappearance'. Remember that episode of *Men Behaving Badly*, with the insufferable posh student who keeps on talking about anthropological rituals when they go to the pub? That's Adam O'Riordan, at his worst.

When we find a character in a later poem 'raising his phone like a chasuble', we see again the attempt to generate significance by falling back on a lexicon of significance, without any searching-out of complexity. And somewhere else, talking about an image from a news story, we have 'There is something of the fall, of course'. Of *course*. Further along, he describes a child watching its mother jump into a pool of water, 'and we who watched knew all there was of loss'. Wow. *All* there was, really? The effect is of a poet who feels very far above his material, of someone far too at home in the registers of grand significance. 'We thought you atavistic' he says of his neighbour at some point. Presumably because neighbour didn't know what a chasuble was.

It's a shame, because O'Riordan can turn a decent phrase: in 'The Dark Star' we get 'a gray muscle of rain / flexing on the Pennines'. Elsewhere there's this:

> the trout came
> glistening up
>
> the clockwork
> of its mouth
>
> a miracle

And there are some fine poems here; 'The Devil's Festival' unwinds its images over a fourteen-line sentence, skil-fully arranging its complex grammar to hold back the big reveal. 'Spam' movingly describes receiving spam from the hacked email account of an ex, the familiar address 'A sloughed husk, an empty shell, / hold it to your ear and hear the ocean'. It's precisely in the moments where the poems are allowed to be smaller and less grand that *A Herring Famine* shines.

*

Where O'Riordan comes from a very recognisable British tradition, Olzmann comes from its American equivalent. His wandering, discursive poems, interested in emotional punch and philosophy alike, draw on C. K. Williams, Jane Hirschfield and Timothy Donnelly for their foundations. But there's plenty here that's Olzmann's alone.

There is the sense that these pieces were written for performance, for a start. The poems all come tagged with aids to comprehension: in a poem about building a monument, we get 'Look at it now!' and then, slightly later, 'What does he think as he builds?' This kind of storytelling scaffolding is everywhere in the book; it's always this:

> What do I mean? I mean
> despite everything, we might search
> for something and never find it.

when the same idea would be conveyed without the first half of that passage. Elsewhere he uses such props to jet off in a new, apparently unrelated direction: 'Thing is, he reminds me [...]' or 'Let me tell you about the time [...]' or 'Did I mention [...]'. We're constantly drawn back to the idea of a person speaking. That could be interesting, but the speaking character isn't complexified, fleshed out: it's a young, American poet, mischievous and sad in the way that young American poets are. So it goes.

In this, and in several other ways, Olzmann's not much of a ('page') poet. The only time he departs from his meandering, discursive free verse is for a villanelle which is almost comically bad. He struggles for rhymes after 'the deep / wells of memory from going dry', and comes up with 'The cold sweep / of moonlight. Photographs. Your lover's thigh.' and then 'the beep / of the alarm clock from telling another lie'. Which sounds profound for exactly as long as you refrain from thinking about it.

But here's the thing: this stuff doesn't matter that much. Olzmann *isn't* much of a poet, but he *is* a strong storyteller, a charming narrator and a decent philosopher of ontology. There are two primary themes running through the book: the first is the relationship between the real and the imaginary; the pull that the imagination can have on the realm of the real, cashed out in politics and art and human relationships. The second theme is loss, and in particular the loss of a friend to suicide. Because this latter theme isn't made explicit until section two of the book, there's a moving dawning realisation effected that this is a book of poems about the imaginary – the not-quite-real and the lost – precisely because its narrator is desperately without a lost friend, someone who can only be returned in imagination.

There's a lot that's funny, interesting and touching in *Contradictions in the Design*, and it would be better served if I had more space to write about it. So, although it occasionally strays into the over-padded or the saccharine (I liked Olzmann's presumably accidental homage to Roger McGough in 'After I worked as a telemarketer, and dialed a thousand numbers everyday, / but never heard your voice'), this ends up being a book well worth looking out for.

*

If I told you that by far the best sections of a book of poetry were about old lighthouse keepers and the divorce of a narrator's parents, I'd understand if you didn't believe me. And yet that's true of Miriam Nash's book *All the Prayers in the House*. There's some really skilful and subtle interplay between the poems which allow one extremely well-worn subject – the liminal spaces of coastlines and beaches where the history of lighthouses and shipping intrude – to illuminate another – the emotional stress of someone's parents separating and finding new partners. The crucial poem in this process is called 'Of His Bones', which consists simply in an itemisation of bones found in different places:

> I found his kneecaps
>   nestled
>   with the crabs
>   his vertebrae
>   unstacked

and so on, the indented lines nicely mimicking the tideline, the words scattered bones; the rattling 'caps/crabs/unstacked' half-rhymes setting time. But the poem also has the line 'The seabed is full of fathers', and the presence of that one word 'fathers' changes everything. Without it, this would be a dullish poem; with, it becomes a powerful link between the poems here about the sea and the poems about the departing father. When, a couple of poems later, we come across 'A Lightkeeper Must Be a Man of Parts', the sense of those parts as (amongst other things) bits of skeleton destined inevitably to go to pieces is deeply affecting.

These early poems' interlinkings and half-submerged meditation on the sea and broken fathers and loneliness are definite high point, though, and elsewhere Nash succumbs to a much easier sentimentality. There's the regulation scatter of formal pieces – sonnets, fragmentary sequences, a pantoum, none of which are very deeply thought-through. There's even a villanelle to match Olzmann's in the extravagance of its meaningless deepities:

> You don't need strings for your guitar
> to pluck upon infinity
> but set your measure by a star
>
> that's burning neither near nor far
> (distance is imaginary
> now you ride where the numbers are).

Or, even worse, 'teach us a formula / to map the heart's velocity'. What could that possibly mean? Must we decide what's meant by the heart's 'velocity', and then what it would mean to 'map' a velocity, and then how formulae are relevant to this mapping process? Nash seems to be far less in control of her material than she was in this book's first poems. Perhaps she's a poet of atmosphere, and not one of statement. No shame there, though, and *All the Prayers in the House* contributes a fair few interesting poems to the landscape.

"It is characteristic of literary history to be forgetful of writers who fall outside of its expected patterns. Lola Ridge – poet, anarchist and passionate feminist – should by rights be a name to set next to, though in contrast to, her modernist contemporaries, Gertrude Stein and Marianne Moore."

ANNE STEVENSON

Its Own Reward

Collette Bryce, *Selected Poems* (Picador) £14.99; Sean Wai Keung, *you are mistaken* (The Rialto) £6.99

Reviewed by WILL MACLEAN

There are some poets whose control is overwhelmingly obvious. Opening her *Selected Poems*, Collette Bryce takes on the role of field captain barking commands at her 'line':

> maze through the slating,
> dive from sight and down into history, Line,
> take flight in the chase of the fences,
> leap the streets

If anyone has such authority over their 'Line', it is Bryce. This book selects from her four published collections since the start of the millennium, and it stands as a testament to the possibility of sheer poetic skill. Even when playful and wry, there is a magnificent patterning and precision at work in 'Plot Summary, Scene 4':

> [I would] approach you in a cool embrace and kiss
> alternate zones of your face, solemnly, like a delegate
> from some forgotten independent state
> whose population waits, has staked on this
> all hope.

The 'a' sound in 'embrace' and 'face' lurks around the lines and yet is absent from the eye-rhyme of 'delegate'/'state' where it is most needed. As if to rub in this failure, 'state' is near-rhymed with 'waits' and alliterated with 'staked' in the next line. Her chamber music is so precise as to be able to harmonise its dissonances as well as consonances.

The tightness of sounds in her poems means that when an inspired phrase comes it has an electric zip to it. Postcards land on her floor 'like meteorites' and the 'refuse vehicle's cavernous jaw / reverses massively out of an avenue'. The same is true for the moments of hard-won uncertainty: 'Aloneness / is the word I was looking for.'

Yet her control can become tiring. Bryce is electrifying in small doses; in a career-spanning collection it's perhaps too much. She occasionally seems overly proud of the intricacy of her allegories and conceits, wanting to show them off to make sure we *get* it. 'Self-portrait in a Broken Mirror' would be far better without expository comments such as:

> But no, that's me, a cubist depiction [...]

Perhaps she acknowledges this. In 'A Spider' she has

> [...] trapped a spider in a glass,
> a fine-blown wineglass.

We sometimes feel like this spider, trapped in the delicate 'glass' of her poems, within a '*wall that is there but not there*'. Yet her willingness to acknowledge this does not remedy the fault. She is at her best when she reaches out of the wineglass and into something bigger. Given the intricacies and wars in her Northern-Irish upbringing, there can be far less hand-holding in her magisterial poem 'Derry':

> I slowly grew to understand
>
> the way the grey Cathedral cast
>   its shadow on our learning, cool,
> as sunlight crept from east to west.

Understand what about it exactly? Bryce's undoubted talent fares better when such a question remains unanswered.

Sean Wai Keung's debut pamphlet, *you are mistaken*, is more content than Bryce to enjoy 'allowing yourself to be driven / by forces beyond your control'. These poems are frequently informed by Wai Keung's Chinese heritage (he writes a sonnet sequence on different Chinese characters), yet his writing is equally informed by exploring and condensing financial instability and mental uncertainty: 'i dont always follow my own principles that would completely defeat the point of having them'.

Self-contradiction and self-doubt are the prevailing moods of this writing, evoked by Wai Keung's remarkable ear for the blackly comic which punctures any surface level of assurance. In 'stealing table sauces from wetherspoons' he remarks upon:

> the safe knowledge that with enough
> condiments any meal is edible

Such a comment prompts laughter that cannot mask the lived struggle and want beneath. Sometimes, when we laugh it is to echo his contempt:

> i think about winning awards
> for my poems or for being
> a good human being

The high point of an impressive pamphlet is 'i think i want to write about race', which represents one-half of a conversation with an anonymous interlocutor who somehow manages to be everyone. It showcases Wai Keung's outstanding awareness of patronising pockets of language and lays bare what he elsewhere recognises as 'asian racism':

> have you read sarah howe
> you should ask for funding so you can go back to hongkong
> o thats actually pretty interesting
> great move thats what the arts council like

Occasionally the writing *you are mistaken* seems a touch rambling, but it is more than redeemed by the steely incisiveness of moments like this. If it doesn't make a white reader of poetry uncomfortable then they are not listening hard enough. I anticipate his future work with excitement and not a little disquiet.

Negative Capability

Dan Beachy-Quick, *Of Silence and Song* (Milkweed Editions) £9.99

Reviewed by VALERIE DUFF

American poet Dan Beachy-Quick is no stranger to an ambitious project. His latest *Of Silence and Song*, which is not wholly poetry, memoir, essay or history, begins by plunging into the negative: 'On our walk my youngest daughter asked me, 'What are the songs you don't know?' His answer: 'Silence was the best description.' *Of Silence and Song* devotes itself to this riddle, in search of where world and absence meet.

But this is a book not *comprised* of silence ultimately; it is one that calls *attention* to stillness and record. It is a book of histories and legends that have come to rest in silence and retelling. Of actions that can only be met with silence. But it is mostly about wandering. Using leitmotifs as guide, Beachy-Quick gives himself license to wander, ranging as far as Duchamp, the Greek muse Tacita, Paul Celan's changing name ('in anagram a kind of diaspora'), to the glint of the helmets in *The Iliad*. Ending on various pilgrimages with his family (to Rome, etc), the book is a preserver of relics. The things surrounded by silence are realised in minutiae (a young child's sleep rituals, the pressed flowers left in Emily Dickinson's bible, nails from Thoreau's cabin). *Of Song and Silence* leans on the labyrinth of classical thought, from the origin of Hebrew letters and the story of Homer's life, into the deepest modern quagmires of race violence, gun control and climate change.

Beachy-Quick is a poet, and there are poems laced throughout, but his prose only needs them as addition, accumulation, run-off from the previous meditation. He knows his Western Canon, with the precision of Euclid somewhere in the background. The lyricism of the essays may make the book a poem entire – if the geometric definition of a point can be compared to a poem: 'that which has no part' yet is oxymoronically the thing itself, the underpinning of all. Beachy-Quick reminds us all is held together by memory, 'that shield called mind'.

This is a book of strange entries, of existence and the recording of that existence: 'To know that you do not know. Can it be more than a riddle? To know and also not know what you know. To live within it as one would live within a plot. I don't mean a narrative. I mean a small space just big enough for your body, a square of grass, a grave. / As a child I helped my grandfather tend the graves.'

This is a beautiful book, heady in all senses of the word, that delightfully blurs the line and lines of poetry.

From the Archive

Issue 141, September–October 2001

SUJATA BHATT

From a contribution of five 'Self-Portrait' poems alongside 'Self-portrait with a Wreath of Red Flowers in Your Hair'. Fellow contributors to this issue include Simon Armitage, Ruth Padel, Neil Astley, Gabriel Josipovici and Roger Scruton.

SELF-PORTRAIT WITH YELLOWISH GREEN

Parrot green, lime green,
    pistachio green,

yellowish green – bright
on your chin where your hand rests,
the left hand again –
    And there across your eyelids
        more green –

Is it the light?
Or shall I call it a shadow?

Your ears are dark pink: sunburnt, stubborn –

Colours of madness, people will say,
    colours of insanity –

But if you tell them what you really think
they will turn away, afraid –

A Winning Suit

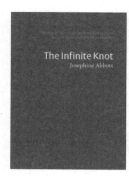

Josephine Abbott, *The Infinite Knot* (Smith/Doorstop) £5; Lesley Saunders, *Angels on Horseback* (S/D) £5; Katy Evans-Bush, *Broken Cities* (S/D) £5; Ruth McIlroy, *Guppy Primer* (S/D) £5; Maya Catherine Popa, *The Bees Have Been Canceled* (Southword) £7.99

Reviewed by JANE DRAYCOTT

A strong poetry pamphlet can make for an absorbing studio-scale unity of work, charged with all the wider vision of the artist in a space small enough to reveal detailed echoes across its framework. Josephine Abbot's *The Infinite Knot* (a winner of the 2017 Poetry Business Competition) formalises exactly that potential in a set of twenty-one meditative lyrics reflecting symmetrically across a central, eleventh poem, a transformative account of a pair of swallows:

> they fell together, sychnronised,
>   sure of never falling,
> and took us with them. Air breathed
>   through the tips of our fingers

Abbott's fine-touch exploration of a long and close relationship finds a distillation point again in a second bird poem, about two white swans 'symmetrical as bedside lamps' that 'reflect each other exactly, faithfully. // Their stillness is catching'. It's a sequence patterned with images of water and flight and fire in a ricochet of quiet resonance whose delicacy extends even to the titling of the poems, simply numbered *i* to *xi* and back, a mirroring architecture that gives *The Infinite Knot* a highly personal and singular integrity.

Lesley Saunders' *Angels on Horseback* (also a 2017 Poetry Business winner) is a sensuous, dramatic investigation into fragile and violent female experience: 'In her mind she serves them other delicacies – rashers of their own hearts, diced brains, gelatinous eyes – on the plate of herself' ('Twelve Little Murders and a Bird Feeder'). It's a work of impressive imaginative vitality, an energy achieved partly through the characteristic intricacy of Saunders' imagery and feel for the glories of rare vocabulary ('the ghosts of shoes / mouse-like and papery, wag-wantons, tottergrass'), but also through the collection's subtlety of animating thought and feeling. Images of cover-up, things withheld or shallow-buried, recur as the coolly attentive language probes beneath surface narratives, uncovering a variety of unsettling and vivid associations with myth and fable:

> Alone and stripped, her sister is waiting there in the flesh,
> in the flowerless underworld, with lapis lazuli and lanterns.
>   ('The Shy Woman').

Eight of the most dramatic poems are part of a collaboration with Susan Adams, a fascinating visual artist whose fantastical aesthetic Saunders shares with compelling results.

There's a spiky energy also in the poetics of Ruth McIlroy's *Guppy Primer,* a fresh and striking first pamphlet that is a PBS Pamphlet Choice as well as Poetry Business winner alongside Saunders, Abbott and Katy Evans-Bush. Dark and darkly playful, McIlroy's work reaches for lyrical expression in a searching range of phrasal experimentation: 'some scraps of old song-lines and sayings / On the tip of my tongue: yes, like that, no not that' – an extract from 'Gaps', a manifesto poem about the pulse of a strobing lighthouse which also contains the beautifully choreographed:

> 'It was,   , stars,   , stars,   , stars,   ;
> [...]
> (There was dream, not dream, beam, not beam, dream not dream, beam).

Charged by ideas of contraction and incompleteness, *Guppy Primer* is quickened too by sharp humour, set ticking in the leading poem 'Will you be my Bridesmaid': 'and if you are unwilling / I will leave you alone at a different table / and I will laugh with my mates / and you will have no mates // you are / the jewel / in my'. Hard to believe this is a debut pamphlet.

Katy Evans-Bush's prize-winning *Broken Cities* is her fourth collection, delivered with all her trademark wryness and invention. Her subject is breakdown, change and decay – within cities, London in particular, and within the body and the self – observed in often brightly surreal and luminous detail: 'Little back specks fly in from the garden / [...] come to rest in planetary seas / that form round volcanic islands of rotting meat' ('Wise Guys Lounge'). Two fine elegiac poems early in the collection attest to Evans-Bush's assured sense of timing and musicality in both rhyme and free verse:

> He rests his head back. He sits. There is a clot in his heart,
> on its splendid red throne among the gold-tipped dignitaries.
>   ('The Great Illness')

All in *Broken Cities* seems suspended, under threat, yet Evans-Bush fires up her sharpened response with a resistant pleasure in language, not least in the fine 'To the Sea Party', ringing with wonderful strangeness: 'The noctiluca / [...] are both canapé / and Chinese lantern. It's their party. Down here / you eat the prey that shines, while you shine on your prey.'

Resistance of a different kind informs the poetics of New York poet Maya Catherine Popa's *The Bees Have Been Canceled,* winner of the Gregory O'Donoghue International Prize 2017. Poised and powerful, the poems are shot through with strong feeling both personal and political in their restless, condensed narratives: 'suddenly there's you // by the haystacks holding a bridle. Or is that the writer again/fawning on a feeling, dreaming of wool's division into further wool'. Popa's is above all a thoughtful voice 'burdened & amplified by knowledge' and worried. 'I worry // for the seasons which cannot / worry for each other', she writes in 'Uranium in English', a key sequence considering how such issues as nuclear arms, industrial farming and gun culture can be approached within a classroom – 'I teach my class / the problem /

solution structure [...] // what does being right look like?' Questions persist: 'What do we know of this tilting life?' asks the poet in 'The End of the World Has Been Canceled', and answers in typically generative terms:

light the rift between

tomorrow, no tomorrow,

two movies competing
for the same ticket.

From the Archive

Issue 141, September–October 2001

ROGER SCRUTON

From an essay exploring the anthroponomastics of poetry. Fellow contributors to this issue include Simon Armitage, Ruth Padel, Neil Astley, Gabriel Josipovici and Sujata Bhatt.

WHAT'S IN A NAME?

An important part of every writer's task is to use proper names judiciously. Shakespeare's names – Ophelia, Prospero, Caliban, Portia, Bottom, Titania, Malvolio – summon character and plot, and also seem to light up regions of the human psyche, so that we can say, knowing what we mean and without other words to express it, 'I am not Prince Hamlet, nor was meant to be'. And what poem makes greater use of a name than the one from which I have just quoted? 'The Love Song of J. Alfred Prufrock': all the existential hesitation of the protagonist is foreshadowed in the title, which illustrates the deep-down impossibility of anyone called J. Alfred Prufrock uttering a plausible love song. Christopher Ricks shows this with characteristic *élan* in *T.S. Eliot and Prejudice*: '"I'm in love", "Who's the lucky man?", "J. Alfred Prufrock" – impossible.'

SOME CONTRIBUTORS

Duncan MacKay is a Senior Research Fellow at the Centre for Astrophysics & Planetary Science, University of Kent, Canterbury – also engaged in research at the Centre for Modern Poetry in the School of English.

James Womack is a translator and poet who lives in Cambridge, where he teaches Spanish and English. His second collection, *On Trust: A Book of Lies*, was published in 2017.

Vahni Capildeo's latest book is *Venus as a Bear* (Carcanet, 2018; Poetry Book Society Summer Choice). Capildeo is the Douglas Caster Cultural Fellow in Poetry at the University of Leeds.

Parwana Fayyaz was born in Kabul, Afghanistan, and studied CompLit and Creative Writing at Stanford University. She is doing a PhD in Persian Studies at the University of Cambridge.

Barry Wood retired in 2004 and currently enjoys an honorary fellowship at MMU and tutors for MANCENT. His interests include modern poetry, translation and the short story. He reads much of the night, spends as much time as possible with his granddaughter, and tries not to think about Trump.

Jamie Osborn lives in Brussels. He has published translations of Iraqi refugee poems in *Modern Poetry in Translation* and elsewhere, and his poems appear in *New Poetries VII* (Carcanet).

Ashley Anna McHugh won the 2010 *New Criterion* Prize with her debut collection, *Into These Knots*. Her poems have appeared in *Nimrod*, *Measure* and *The Hopkins Review*, among other venues.

Maryann Corbett is the author of four books of poetry, most recently *Street View*, from Able Muse Press. She is a past winner of the Richard Wilbur Award and the Willis Barnstone Translation Prize. One of her poems will appear in *The Best American Poetry 2018*.

Vidyan Ravinthiran is the author of *Grun-tu-molani* (Bloodaxe, 2014), shortlisted for a few prizes, and *Elizabeth Bishop's Prosaic* (Bucknell UP, 2015), winner of both the

University English Prize and the Warren-Brooks Award for Outstanding Literary Criticism. He is an editor at Prac Crit and teaches at Birmingham University.

Craig Raine's last book was *My Grandmother's Glass Eye: A Look at Poetry* (Atlantic Books).

Mark Valentine is the author of *Psammomancy* (Seacliff Press), with music by Brian Lavelle, and *Star Kites* (Tartarus Press).

Nicholas Friedman's first collection, *Petty Theft*, won the *New Criterion* Poetry Prize and will be published in fall 2018. Friedman is a Jones Lecturer in Poetry at Stanford University.

Leo Boix is an Argentinean poet based in the UK. He has published two collections in Spanish and was included in the anthology *Ten: Poets of the New Generation* (Bloodaxe). His English poems have appeared in *MPT*, *The Rialto*, *Magma Poetry*, *The Morning Star* and elsewhere. He is a fellow of The Complete Works Program.

James McGonigal is a Glasgow-based poet and critic, friend and biographer of Edwin Morgan and co-editor of *The Midnight Letterbox* (Carcanet, 2015), a selection of his correspondence 1950–2010.

Fiona Moore's first collection *The Distal Point* will be published by HappenStance Press in July 2018. She is co-editing an issue of *Magma* on climate change.

Kristín Ómarsdóttir is an award-winning Icelandic poet, novelist, short story writer and playwright. Her selected poems, *Waitress in Fall*, is forthcoming from Carcanet in July 2018.

Vala Thorodds is an Iceland-born poet, publisher, editor, translator and literary curator. She is the founding director of Partus, a dual language, independent literary press based in Reykjavík and Manchester.

Alison Brackenbury's *Selected Poems* will be published by Carcanet in February 2019.

Tony Roberts's book of essays, *The Taste in My Mind*, appeared in 2015. His fifth poetry collection, *The Noir American & Other Poems*, will appear this spring. Both are from Shoestring Press.

Jane Draycott's most recent collections are *The Occupant* (Carcanet 2016, PBS Recommendation), and *Storms Under the Skin: Selected Poems of Henri Michaux 1927–1954* (Two Rivers Press 2017, PBS Recommended Translation).

Sasha Dugdale's fourth collection *Joy* was a PBS Choice and the title poem was awarded a Forward Prize for Best Single Poem in 2016. She is former editor of *Modern Poetry in Translation*.

Adam Heardman is a poet and writer from the North-East. His poems have appeared in *PN Review*, *Belleville Park Pages*, *The Missing Slate*, and have been awarded the Mapleton-Bree Prize for the Creative Arts by Oxford University and a Truman Capote Scholarship in the US. He lives and works in Newcastle upon Tyne.

Phoebe Power's debut collection, *Shrines of Upper Austria* (Carcanet) is a Poetry Book Society Recommendation for Spring 2018.

Sue Leigh's new collection of poems, *Chosen Hill*, is published this year by Two Rivers Press. She also teaches part-time at Rewley House, Oxford University's department for continuing education.

--- COLOPHON ---

Editors
Michael Schmidt (General)
Andrew Latimer (Deputy)

Editorial address
The Editors at the address on the right. Manuscripts cannot be returned unless accompanied by a stamped addressed envelope or international reply coupon.

Trade distributors
NBN International
10 Thornbury Road
Plymouth PL6 7PP, UK
orders@nbninternational.com

Design
Luke Allan
Typeset by Little Island Press in Arnhem Pro.

Represented by
Compass IPS Ltd
Great West House
Great West Road, Brentford
TW8 9DF, UK
sales@compass-ips.london

Copyright
© 2018 Poetry Nation Review
All rights reserved
ISBN 978-1-78410-152-7
ISSN 0144-7076

Subscriptions (6 issues)
INDIVIDUALS (print and digital): £39.50; abroad £49.00
INSTITUTIONS (print only): £56.00; abroad £70.00
INSTITUTIONS (digital): subscriptions from Exact Editions (https://shop.exacteditions.com/gb/pn-review)
to: *PN Review*, Alliance House 30 Cross Street, Manchester M2 7AQ, UK

Supported by